brunch

SUSANNAH BLAKE

LORENZ BOOKS

For all recipes, **quantities** are given in both **metric** & **imperial** measures &, where appropriate, measures' are also given in **standard cups** & **spoons**. Follow one set, but not a mixture, because they are **not interchangeable**.

Standard **spoon** & **cup measures** are level.
1 tsp = 5ml, 1 tbsp = 15ml, 1 cup = 250 ml/8fl oz

Australian standard **tablespoons** are 20ml. Australian readers should use 3 tsp in place of 1 tbsp for measuring small quantities of gelatine, sugar, flour, salt, etc.

Medium (US large) eggs are used unless otherwise stated.

Bracketed terms are intended for **American** readers.

This edition is published by Lorenz Books
Lorenz Books is an imprint of Anness Publishing Ltd
Hermes House, 88–89 Blackfriars Road, London SE1 8HA
tel. 020 7401 2077; fax 020 7633 9499
www.lorenzbooks.com; info@anness.com

© Anness Publishing Ltd 2001, 2003

This edition distributed in the UK by The Manning Partnership Ltd,
tel. 01225 478 444; fax 01225 478 440; sales@manning-partnership.co.uk
This edition distributed in the USA and Canada by National Book Network, tel.
301 459 3366; fax 301 459 1705; www.nbnbooks.com
This edition distributed in Australia by Pan Macmillan Australia,
tel. 1300 135 113; fax 1300 135 103; customer.service@macmillan.com.au
This edition distributed in New Zealand by David Bateman Ltd,
tel. (09) 415 7664; fax (09) 415 8892

A CIP catalogue record for this book is available from the British Library.
Publisher: Joanna Lorenz
Managing Editor: Linda Fraser
Editor: Susannah Blake
Design: Norma Martin
Photography: Nicki Dowey, Amanda Heywood, William Lingwood, Thomas Odulate, Sam Stowell
Recipes: Mary Banks, Alex Barker, Nicola Graimes, Maggie Mayhew, Jennie Shapter. Kate Whiteman
Production Controller: Darren Price

10 9 8 7 6 5 4 3 2 1

brunch

introduction

Brunch is the perfect meal for **lazy** weekends and **relaxed** holidays. Take your time over this informal, **late** morning meal – **read** the newspaper or enjoy spending time with your friends and family. Brunch is the perfect indulgence and can **include** just about **anything** – from light and healthy fresh **fruit** salads with yogurt to **eggs** and **bacon** or **freshly** baked bagels filled with cream **cheese**.

the perfect brunch

BRUNCH CAN BE A **MEAL FOR ONE**, A CASUAL **FAMILY AFFAIR**, OR A GREAT EXCUSE TO INVITE FRIENDS OVER. WITH A LITTLE **PLANNING**, YOU CAN ENSURE THAT YOU CAN REALLY **RELAX** AND **ENJOY** YOUSELF AND, WHETHER IT'S JUST YOU OR A GROUP OF **FRIENDS** AND FAMILY, YOUR BRUNCH IS **GUARANTEED** TO BE A **SUCCESS**.

Brunch is a late morning meal that can take the place of breakfast and lunch. It is wonderfully informal and draws its influences from both meals. For a quiet and lazy brunch for one, simply take a tray with coffee, croissants and rich fruity jam back to bed with a good book or a pile of newspapers. Alternatively, you can really go to town: invite guests, plan an extravagant menu and make it a real social event. Whichever you choose – whether it's a simple brunch for one or a luxurious meal for eight – a little forethought will ensure that your brunch is pure, indulgent relaxation for all concerned.

WHERE TO EAT

The beauty of brunch is that you can eat it just about anywhere – in bed, in the kitchen, sprawled on the living room rug, even while lounging in a hot, steamy bath. The only thing to keep in mind is where will you feel relaxed. If you are feeding family or inviting guests, think about where they will be most at home – would they prefer to eat in the dining room, sit around a cosy kitchen table or relax on a sofa with food spread out on a coffee table? *Al fresco* brunching is a great option for warm sunny weather and is perfect for family parties as children can play and run around in the sunshine, leaving the adults to relax and enjoy delicous food and good conversation.

THE MENU

If you're making brunch for one or two, simply choose your favourite foods. When cooking for a group, try to work the menu around your guests and where you have decided to eat. For example, if there will be small children, choose foods that both they and their parents will enjoy. If you're eating outside, choose dishes that can be carried easily and that do not require a lot of time in the kitchen.

Drinks If you invite guests, prepare a choice of cold and hot drinks, such as a jug (pitcher) of fruit juice and a big pot of coffee and/or tea. Offer plenty of cups and glasses so that they can help themselves.

Brunch is a great time to indulge and make breakfast drinks that you wouldn't usually have time to prepare. If you own a juice extractor, create your own special blend of fresh fruit or vegetable juice, or make fresh fruit smoothies and serve straight from the blender. For hot drinks, whip up frothy cappuccinos or caffè lattes, or make steaming cups of rich hot chocolate.

Food You can make just one dish but, to really indulge, choose a selection of foods or dishes that you and/or your guests can pick and choose from. Select dishes that complement each other and that offer a balance of flavours and textures: sweet and savoúry, light and hearty, rich and refreshing, and simple and complex. A good combination might include refreshing fruit salad, a savoury cooked dish such as a soufflé or an omelette, and baked foods such as English muffins, crumpets or rolls with plenty of butter and jam.

INSTANT BRUNCHES

Sometimes the best brunches are those that take no effort at all. Most supermarkets sell a wonderful selection of brunch foods and drinks such as freshly baked bagels, flaky pain au chocolat, ready-made fruit salads, yogurt and freshly squeezed fruit juices. What could be more indulgent than buying a selection of brunch treats the day before, slipping out of bed, loading up a tray and relaxing for an hour or two over such a simple meal.

brunch basics

THERE ARE MANY **SIMPLE DISHES** THAT ARE PERFECT FOR BRUNCH. THEY USE **BASIC INGREDIENTS** AND CAN BE MADE IN MINUTES. CHOOSE **ONE OR TWO** OF THE FOLLOWING AND SERVE WITH **FRUIT JUICE**, COFFEE OR **TEA**, AND PLENTY OF HOT **BUTTERED TOAST**.

BOILED EGGS To make soft-boiled (soft-cooked) eggs, use a tablespoon to lower the eggs into a pan of simmering water. Heat the water until bubbling gently and cook the eggs for about 4 minutes.

POACHED EGGS Pour 4cm/1½in water into a frying pan and bring to the boil. (Do not add salt to the water as this encourages the eggs to spread.) Reduce the heat so that the water is bubbling gently. Crack a very fresh egg into a cup, gently tip into the water (add more eggs in the same way) and cook for 1 minute, spooning water over the yolk(s). When the egg can be easily loosened from the base of the pan, use a slotted spoon to lift the egg(s) from the water and pat dry with kitchen paper.

FRIED EGGS Pour about 30ml/2 tbsp oil into a frying pan. Heat over a medium heat, then crack a fresh egg into the pan (add more eggs in the same way) and cook for about 1 minute. Spoon hot oil over the yolk(s) and cook for 1 minute more until the white has become completely opaque and the edges are turning brown. If you prefer a firmer yolk, cook the egg for a further minute. Use a fish slice (spatula) to lift the egg(s) from the pan.

SCRAMBLED EGGS Allow 2 eggs per person. Break the eggs into a bowl, season with salt and ground black pepper and lightly beat with a fork. Heat 15g/½oz/1 tbsp butter in a small pan until sizzling, then pour in the beaten eggs and stir over a medium heat for 1–2 minutes until the eggs are lightly set but still moist and creamy. For firmer eggs, cook for 1 minute more.

OMELETTES To make a classic omelette for one, break 3 eggs into a bowl, season and beat lightly. Heat 15g/½oz/1 tbsp butter in an omelette pan, then pour in the eggs, tilting the pan. Cook for a few seconds, then push in the cooked sides with a fork and allow the unset egg to run on to the pan. Cook for 1 minute until the egg begins to set. Use a spatula to fold over a third of the omelette, then flip it over again and slide on to a warmed plate.

BACON This can be grilled (broiled) or fried. When cooking whole rashers (strips), cut off the rind with a pair of scissors, then snip the fat at regular intervals to prevent the rashers curling up.

To grill bacon, preheat the grill (broiler), lay the bacon rashers on a rack and grill for 4–8 minutes, turning once.
To fry bacon, grease a frying pan with a very little oil. Heat the pan until hot, then lay the bacon rashers in the pan and fry over a medium-high heat for 4–8 minutes turning once.

SAUSAGES These can be grilled (broiled) or fried. They should always be cooked gently and thoroughly, allowing them to cook right through and become deliciously crisp on the outside.

To grill sausages, preheat the grill (broiler), then place the sausages on a rack and cook well away from the heat source. Cook for about 10 minutes, turning often, until evenly browned.
To fry sausages, pour a little oil into a frying pan. Heat over a medium-low heat, then add the sausages. Cook for 10 minutes, turning occasionally, until cooked through and evenly browned.

KIPPERS

The easiest way to prepare kippers (smoked herrings) is to put them, head down, into a deep bowl, pour over boiling water and leave for 10 minutes, by which time they will be ready to eat.

drinks

zingy vegetable **juice**	12
morning **cleanser**	12
oaty **fruit** smoothie	12
citrus shake	12
banana & **maple** flip	14
prairie oyster	14
buck's **fizz**	16
blackberry & **champagne** crush	16
caffè latte	18
coffee **frappé**	18
cappuccino	18
mexican hot **chocolate**	19

zingy vegetable juice

GINGER PACKS A POWERFUL PUNCH AND CERTAINLY **GETS YOU GOING** IN THE MORNING, EVEN IF YOU'RE FEELING GROGGY. BRIGHTLY COLOURED **CARROTS** AND BEETROOT ARE PACKED WITH **ANTIOXIDANTS**.

ingredients

1 **cooked beetroot** (beet)

1 large **carrot**, sliced

4cm/1½in piece **fresh root ginger**, finely grated

2 **apples**, chopped and cored

150g/5oz/1¼ cups **seedless white grapes**

300ml/½ pint/1¼ cups **fresh orange juice**

method

SERVES 2

1 Place the beetroot, carrot, ginger, apples, grapes and orange juice in a food processor or blender and process for a few minutes until thoroughly combined and fairly smooth. Serve immediately or chill until ready to serve.

morning cleanser

FLAVOURED WITH FRESH GINGER, THIS **CLEANSING** JUICE OFFERS A FINE BALANCE OF **SWEET AND SOUR** FLAVOURS.

ingredients

4 **eating apples**

600ml/1 pint/2½ cups **cranberry juice**

2.5cm/1in piece **fresh root ginger**, peeled and sliced

> **cook's tip**
> If you prefer a smoother juice, strain the processed fruit mixture through a fine sieve before serving. Remember, straining the juice will reduce its fibre content.

method

SERVES 4

1 Peel the apples, if you like, then core and chop. Pour the cranberry juice into a food processor or blender. Add the chopped apples and sliced ginger and process for a few minutes until combined and fairly smooth. Serve chilled.

oaty fruit smoothie

BRIMMING WITH **ENERGY-GIVING** OATS AND FRUITS, THIS **TASTY** DRINK MAKES A **BRILLIANT** BREAKFAST. **LIVE YOGURT** IS GREAT FOR THE DIGESTION.

ingredients

2 **bananas**, quartered

250g/9oz/2¼ cups **strawberries**

30ml/2 tbsp **oatmeal**

600ml/1 pint/2½ cups **natural** (plain) **live yogurt**

method

SERVES 2

1 Place the bananas, strawberries, oatmeal and yogurt in a food processor or blender and process for a few minutes until combined and creamy. Pour into tall glasses and serve.

citrus shake

PACKED WITH HEALTH-GIVING **VITAMIN C**, THIS REFRESHING, **ZESTY** JUICE IS THE PERFECT WAY TO **GET YOU GOING** AT THE BEGINNING OF THE DAY.

ingredients

1 **pineapple**

6 **oranges**, peeled and chopped

juice of 1 **lemon**

1 **pink grapefruit**, peeled and quartered

method

SERVES 4

1 Cut the bottom and the spiky top off the pineapple. Stand it upright and cut off the skin. Lay it on its side and cut into bitesize chunks.

2 Place the pineapple, oranges, lemon juice and grapefruit in a food processor or blender and process for a few minutes until combined.

3 Press the fruit juice through a sieve to remove any pith or membranes. Serve chilled.

banana & maple flip

THIS **NOURISHING** BREAKFAST **DRINK** IS PACKED WITH SO MUCH **GOODNESS** THAT YOU WON'T NEED ANYTHING ELSE FOR YOUR **MORNING MEAL**. AS IT IS MADE WITH A **RAW EGG**, DO BE SURE TO USE A REALLY FRESH ORGANIC ONE.

ingredients

1 small **banana**, peeled and halved

50ml/2fl oz/¼ cup thick **Greek** (US strained plain) **yogurt**

1 **egg**

30ml/2 tbsp **maple syrup**

5ml/1 tsp **lemon juice**

2 **ice cubes**

slice of orange, to serve (optional)

method

SERVES 1

1 Put the banana, yogurt, egg, maple syrup, lemon juice and the ice cubes into a food processor or blender.

2 Blend continuously for about 2 minutes until the mixture becomes really pale and frothy.

3 Pour into a tall, chilled glass and top with a slice of orange to serve, if you like.

variation

There are any number of fruit variations of this delicious, creamy drink. Any of the following fruits can be used in place of the banana: a small, very ripe, peeled, stoned (pitted) and chopped mango; 2 peeled, pitted and chopped peaches or nectarines; or 115g/4oz/1 cup hulled strawberries.

---

prairie oyster

THIS SPICY DRINK IS BASED ON THE ORIGINAL **HANGOVER** REMEDY. IT ALSO TASTES GOOD WITH A SMALL **SPLASH** OF **BRANDY**, AND YOU CAN, OF COURSE, OMIT THE RAW **EGG YOLK**.

ingredients

5ml/1 tsp **Worcestershire sauce**

5ml/1 tsp **white wine vinegar**

5ml/1 tsp **tomato ketchup** or **tomato sauce**

1 **egg yolk**, unbroken

cayenne pepper

method

SERVES 1

1 Place the Worcestershire sauce, white wine vinegar and tomato ketchup or tomato sauce in a tall, narrow glass and mix together using a long-handled spoon or stirrer.

2 Carefully slide the unbroken egg yolk into the glass but do not stir. Sprinkle in a little cayenne pepper and drink in one go.

watchpoint

The very young, the elderly, pregnant women and those in ill-health or with a compromised immune system are advised against consuming raw eggs or dishes and drinks containing raw eggs. This is because salmonella bacteria, which can cause severe food poisoning, are sometimes found in eggs and poultry. The bacteria are destroyed when eggs are heated to a temperature of 60°C/140°F.

buck's fizz

THIS CHAMPAGNE **PICK-ME-UP**, DEVISED AT BUCK'S CLUB, LONDON, WAS ORIGINALLY MADE WITH BOLLINGER CHAMPAGNE, BUT YOU COULD USE ANY **SPARKLING WINE** FOR A MORE ECONOMICAL VERSION.

ingredients

250ml/8fl oz/1 cup **Champagne**
   or **sparkling white**
   wine, chilled
120ml/4fl oz/½ cup freshly
   squeezed **orange juice**

method

SERVES 2

1 Pour the Champagne or sparkling wine into 2 chilled champagne flutes or wine glasses.

2 Add the orange juice, stir very gently, if you like, and then serve immediately while still fizzy.

---

variation

To make a Bellini, fill a wine glass with crushed ice, pour in 50ml/2fl oz/¼ cup peach juice, add a dash of grenadine and top up with chilled Champagne.

---

blackberry & champagne crush

THIS **WONDERFULLY DECADENT** BRUNCH COCKTAIL HAS A JEWEL-LIKE COLOUR AND A BEAUTIFUL **PINKISH-PURPLE** FROTH. THE COMBINATION OF SWEET BLACKBERRIES AND SPARKLING CHAMPAGNE IS **IRRESISTIBLE**.

ingredients

300g/11oz/2¾ cups
   blackberries, chilled
30ml/2 tbsp **icing**
   (confectioners') **sugar**,
   or to taste
60ml/4 tbsp **brandy**
250ml/8fl oz/1 cup **Champagne**
   or **sparkling white**
   wine, chilled

method

SERVES 2

1 Put the blackberries in a food processor and process to a smooth purée. Place a sieve over a bowl and press through it to remove the seeds. Sweeten to taste with icing sugar.

2 Divide the brandy between 2 glasses. Return the blackberry purée to the food processor, add the Champagne or sparkling wine and process for 2–3 seconds. Pour into the glasses and serve immediately.

---

variation

For a brunch party, divide the blackberry purée between 6 Champagne glasses. Pour on chilled Champagne and serve immediately.

caffè latte

THIS IS A VERY **BASIC** BREAKFAST DRINK, AS SERVED IN HOMES AND BARS THROUGHOUT **ITALY** AND **FRANCE**. IT CAN BE MADE WITH ONLY A MANUAL ESPRESSO POT AND A PAN TO HEAT THE MILK.

ingredients

150ml/¼ pint/⅔ cup **espresso** or **very strong coffee**

450ml/¾ pint/scant 2 cups **boiled milk**

sugar (optional)

steamed, frothed milk for topping (optional)

method   SERVES 2

1 Pour the brewed coffee into glasses or large French coffee bowls. Add the hot milk and sugar, if using, and stir well.

2 Top each glass with a spoonful of steamed, frothed milk if you like.

variation
You can flavour the milk by placing a vanilla pod (bean) in it and leaving to infuse (steep) for 10 minutes. Remove the vanilla pod before using the milk.

coffee frappé

SIMILAR TO A **MILK-SHAKE**, THIS ICY FRAPPÉ IS A LONG, **COLD** COFFEE **DRINK** THAT IS BOTH REFRESHING AND **UPLIFTING**.

variation
There are countless variations on the classic frappé. Try using chocolate, maple or almond essence in place of the vanilla essence.

ingredients

450ml/¾ pint/scant 2 cups **cold strong coffee** (brewed using about 80g/3¼oz/1 cup coffee per 1 litre/1¾ pints/4 cups of water)

8 drops **vanilla essence** (extract)

300ml/½ pint/1¼ cups **crushed ice**

60ml/4 tbsp **sweetened condensed milk**

sugar, to taste

whipped cream and sliced **banana**, to serve (optional)

method   SERVES 2

1 Pour the cold coffee into a food processor or blender.

2 Add the vanilla essence, crushed ice and condensed milk and blend until smooth.

3 Pour into tall glasses and stir in sugar to taste. Top with some whipped cream and banana slices, if you like.

cappuccino

THE **CLASSIC** ITALIAN FROTHY COFFEE.

ingredients

150–250ml/5–8fl oz/⅔–1 cup very cold **whole milk**

about 75ml/2½fl oz/⅓ cup **freshly brewed espresso**

chocolate powder (optional)

method   SERVES 2

1 Pour very cold milk into a metal jug (pitcher) or frothing device, steam until a fine, smooth foam has formed and set aside.

2 Pour the freshly brewed espresso into cappuccino or regular 150ml/5fl oz/⅔ cup coffee cups.

3 Pour the steamed milk over the coffee, holding back the froth with a spoon until last, when it can be spooned on to the surface. Sprinkle a little chocolate powder on top, if you like, and serve.

mexican hot chocolate

MEXICAN CHOCOLATE IS FLAVOURED WITH **ALMONDS**, CINNAMON AND **VANILLA**, AND IS SWEETENED WITH SUGAR. IT COMES IN DISCS AND CAN BE BOUGHT IN SPECIALIST STORES. MEXICAN CHOCOLATE PRODUCES A PARTICULARLY **RICH AND AROMATIC** HOT CHOCOLATE THAT IS PERFECT FOR A **RELAXING** BRUNCH.

ingredients

1 litre/1¾ pints/4 cups **milk**
50–115g/2–4oz **Mexican chocolate** (1–2 discs)
1 **vanilla pod** (bean)

variation
If you like, you can use dark (bittersweet) chocolate instead of Mexican chocolate. You will need slightly less, as the flavour will be more intense.

method

SERVES 4

1 Pour the milk into a pan and add the chocolate. Precisely how much to use will depend on personal taste. Start with 1 disc and use more next time if necessary.

2 Split the vanilla pod lengthways using a sharp knife, and add it to the pan of milk.

3 Heat the chocolate milk gently, stirring until all the chocolate has dissolved, then whisking with a wire whisk until the mixture boils. Remove the vanilla pod and divide the drink among 4 mugs or heatproof glasses. Serve immediately.

cereals, porridge & fruit

luxury muesli

COMMERCIALLY MADE **MUESLI** REALLY CAN'T COMPETE WITH THIS **HOME-MADE** VERSION. THIS COMBINATION OF SEEDS, **GRAINS**, **NUTS** AND DRIED FRUITS WORKS PARTICULARLY WELL, BUT YOU CAN ALTER THE **BALANCE** OF INGREDIENTS, OR SUBSTITUTE OTHERS, IF YOU LIKE.

ingredients

50g/2oz/½ cup **sunflower seeds**

25g/1oz/¼ cup **pumpkin seeds**

115g/4oz/1 cup **rolled oats**

115g/4oz/heaped 1 cup **wheat flakes**

115g/4oz/generous 1 cup **barley flakes**

115g/4oz/1 cup **raisins**

115g/4oz/1 cup chopped **hazelnuts, roasted**

115g/4oz/½ cup **dried apricots**, chopped

50g/2oz/2 cups **dried apple slices**, halved

25g/1oz/⅓ cup **desiccated** (dry unsweetened shredded) **coconut**

method

SERVES 4

1 Put the sunflower and pumpkin seeds in a dry frying pan and cook over a medium heat for 3 minutes until golden, tossing the seeds regularly to prevent them from burning.

2 Mix the toasted seeds with the remaining ingredients and leave to cool. Store in an airtight container.

---

variation
Serve the muesli in a long glass layered with fresh raspberries and fromage frais or cream cheese. Soak the muesli first in a little water or fruit juice in order to soften it slightly.

---

granola

HONEY-COATED NUTS, SEEDS AND **OATS**, COMBINED WITH SWEET **DRIED FRUITS**, MAKE AN EXCELLENT AND **NUTRITIOUS** START TO THE DAY – WITHOUT THE ADDITIVES OFTEN FOUND IN PRE-PACKED CEREALS. SERVE THE GRANOLA WITH SEMI-SKIMMED **MILK** OR NATURAL LIVE **YOGURT** AND FRESH FRUIT.

ingredients

115g/4oz/1 cup **rolled oats**

115g/4oz/1 cup **jumbo oats**

50g/2oz/½ cup **sunflower seeds**

25g/1oz/2 tbsp **sesame seeds**

50g/2oz/½ cup **hazelnuts**, roasted

25g/1oz/¼ cup **almonds**, roughly chopped

50ml/2fl oz/¼ cup **sunflower oil**

50ml/2fl oz/¼ cup **clear honey**

50g/2oz/scant ½ cup **raisins**

50g/2oz/½ cup **dried sweetened cranberries**

method

SERVES 4

1 Preheat the oven to 140ºC/275ºF/Gas 1. Mix together the oats, seeds and nuts in a bowl.

2 Heat the oil and honey in a large pan until melted, then remove the pan from the heat. Add the oat mixture and stir well. Spread out on one or two baking sheets.

3 Bake for about 50 minutes until crisp, stirring occasionally to prevent the mixture from sticking. Remove the baking sheets from the oven and mix in the raisins and cranberries. Leave to cool, then store in an airtight container.

ingredients

50g/2oz/½ cup **whole blanched almonds**

115g/4oz/⅔ cup ready-to-eat **dried apricots**

200g/7oz/2 cups **whole rolled oats**

75g/3oz/2 cups **wheatflakes** or **oatbran flakes**

50g/2oz/scant ½ cup **raisins** or **sultanas** (golden raisins)

40g/1½oz/⅓ cup **pumpkin seeds**

40g/1½oz/⅓ cup **sunflower seeds**

skimmed milk, **low-fat natural** (plain) **yogurt** or **fresh fruit juice**, and **fresh fruit**, to serve

cook's tip
Ring the changes by adding other dried fruits, such as chopped dates, figs, peaches, pear, pineapple or apple chunks. Walnuts, brazil nuts or hazelnuts could be substituted for the almonds.

apricot & almond muesli

THERE IS NO ADDED SUGAR IN THIS TASTY WHOLEWHEAT **FRUIT** AND **NUT** MUESLI, WHICH IS PACKED WITH FIBRE, **VITAMINS** AND MINERALS.

method

SERVES 8

1 Using a sharp knife, carefully cut the almonds into slivers. Cut the dried apricots into small evensize pieces.

2 Stir all the ingredients together in a large bowl. Store in an airtight container and use within 6 weeks.

3 Serve with skimmed milk, natural yogurt or fruit juice and top with fresh fruit, such as peach, banana or strawberry slices.

fruity sesame porridge

OATS ARE INCREDIBLY GOOD FOR YOU AND MAKE A WONDERFULLY **NOURISHING** BRUNCH. THEY PROVIDE PLENTY OF LOW-FAT **ENERGY** THAT IS RELEASED SLOWLY THROUGHOUT THE MORNING. THE ADDITION OF **DRIED FRUIT** AND TOASTED **SESAME** SEEDS MAKE IT EVEN BETTER.

ingredients

50g/2oz/½ cup **rolled oats**
475ml/16fl oz/2 cups
 skimmed milk
75g/3oz/½ cup **ready-to-eat
 dried fruit salad**, chopped
30ml/2 tbsp **sesame
 seeds,** toasted

method

SERVES 2

1 Put the rolled oats, milk and chopped dried fruit in a non-stick pan. Bring to the mixture to boil, then lower the heat and simmer gently for 3 minutes, stirring occasionally, until thickened. Serve in individual bowls, sprinkled with toasted sesame seeds.

cook's tip
If you use "old-fashioned" or "original" oats, the porridge will be quite thick and coarse textured. You could also use jumbo oats. If you prefer a smoother porridge, try ordinary rolled oats (sometimes called oatflakes).

porridge with date purée & pistachios

DATES GIVE A NATURAL **SWEET** FLAVOUR TO THIS **WARMING** AND DELICIOUS WINTER BRUNCH DISH.

ingredients

250g/9oz/scant 2 cups **fresh dates**

475ml/16fl oz/2 cups **semi-skimmed** (low-fat) **milk**

225g/8oz/2 cups **rolled oats**

pinch of **salt**

50g/2oz/½ cup shelled, **unsalted pistachio nuts**, roughly chopped

method

SERVES 4

1 First make the date purée. Halve the dates and remove the stones (pits) and stems. Cover the dates with boiling water and leave to soak for about 30 minutes, until softened. Strain, reserving 90ml/6 tbsp of the soaking water.

2 Remove the skin from the dates and place them in a food processor with the reserved soaking water. Process to a smooth purée.

3 Place the milk and oats in a large pan with 300ml/½ pint/1¼ cups water and the salt. Bring to the boil, then reduce the heat and simmer for 4–5 minutes until cooked and creamy, stirring frequently.

4 Serve the porridge in warm serving bowls, topped with a spoonful of the date purée and sprinkled with chopped pistachio nuts.

variation

To make an apricot purée, use dried apricots in place of the dates. There is no need to remove the skins in step 2, simply purée them. Sprinkle over chopped almonds in place of the pistachio nuts.

apricot & ginger compote

FRESH GINGER ADDS **WARMTH** TO THIS STIMULATING BRUNCH DISH AND **COMPLEMENTS** THE FLAVOUR OF THE PLUMP, JUICY **APRICOTS**.

ingredients

350g/12oz/1½ cups ready-to-eat **dried apricots**

4cm/1½in piece **fresh root ginger**, finely chopped

200g/7oz/scant 1 cup **natural** (plain) **live yogurt** or **fromage frais**

flaked (sliced) **almonds**, toasted, to sprinkle (optional)

method

SERVES 4

1 Put the apricots in a bowl, cover with boiling water, then leave to soak overnight.

2 Place the apricots and their soaking water in a pan, add the ginger and bring to the boil. Reduce the heat and simmer for 10 minutes until the fruit is soft and plump and the water becomes syrupy. Strain the apricots, reserving the syrup, and discard the ginger.

3 Serve the compote warm with the reserved syrup and a spoonful of yogurt or fromage frais. Sprinkle over flaked almonds if you like.

cook's tip

Fresh ginger freezes well. Peel the root and store it in a plastic bag in the freezer. You can grate it from frozen, then return the root to the freezer until the next time you need it for a recipe.

ingredients

For the orange and prune compote

1 **juicy orange**, peeled

50g/2oz/⅓ cup **ready-to-eat prunes**

75ml/5 tbsp **orange juice**

For the pear and kiwi fruit compote

1 **ripe eating pear**, cored

1 **kiwi fruit**

60ml/4 tbsp **apple or pineapple juice**

For the grapefruit and strawberry compote

1 ruby **grapefruit**, peeled

115g/4oz/1 cup **strawberries**

60ml/4 tbsp **orange juice**

To serve

natural (plain) **yogurt** and **toasted hazelnuts**

three fruit compotes

PACKED WITH **VITAMINS** AND WONDERFULLY **REFRESHING**, FRUIT IS AN EXCELLENT WAY TO START THE DAY. **DIFFERENT FRUITS** ALWAYS COMPLEMENT EACH OTHER, SO TRY ANY ONE OF THESE **DELICIOUS** FRUIT **COMBINATIONS** FOR A REAL TREAT.

---

cook's tip

Choose "fresh-pressed" juices rather than those made from concentrates. Alternatively, squeeze your own juice using a food processor or blender.

---

method

EACH COMPOTE SERVES 1

1 To make the orange and prune compote, segment the orange and place in a bowl with the prunes. Pour over the orange juice.

2 To make the pear and kiwi fruit compote, slice the pear, then peel and cut the kiwi fruit into wedges. Place in a bowl and pour over the apple or pineapple juice.

3 To make the grapefruit and strawberry compote, segment the grapefruit and cut the strawberries in half. Place the fruits in a bowl and pour over the orange juice.

4 Serve the compotes topped with a spoonful of natural yogurt sprinkled with chopped toasted hazelnuts.

fresh fig compote

THESE **LUSCIOUS** FRUITS HAVE THE MOST **DELICIOUSLY SUCCULENT** TASTE AND TEXTURE. LIGHTLY POACHING THEM IN A **VANILLA** AND **COFFEE SYRUP** REALLY HELPS TO BRING OUT THEIR WONDERFUL FLAVOUR AND MAKES A **PERFECT BRUNCH**.

method

SERVES 4–6

1 Choose a frying pan with a lid, large enough to hold the figs in a single layer. Pour in the coffee and add the honey.

2 Split the vanilla pod lengthwise with a sharp knife and scrape the tiny black seeds into the pan, with the tip of the knife. Add the vanilla pod, then bring the mixture to the boil. Boil the syrup rapidly until reduced to about 175ml/6fl oz/¾ cup. Remove the pan from the heat and set aside to cool.

3 Wash the figs and pierce the skins several times with a sharp skewer. Cut the fruits in half and add them to the cooled coffee syrup. Cover the pan with a lid and simmer over a low heat for 5 minutes.

4 Remove the figs from the syrup with a slotted spoon, place in a serving dish and set aside to cool.

5 Strain the syrup through a fine sieve straight over the figs. Allow the compote to stand at room temperature for 1 hour before serving. Serve with yogurt, if you like.

ingredients

400ml/14fl oz/1⅔ cups **brewed coffee**
115g/4oz/½ cup **clear honey**
1 **vanilla pod** (bean)
12 **slightly under-ripe fresh figs**
Greek (US strained plain) **yogurt**, to serve (optional)

cook's tips
Rinse and dry the vanilla pod; it can be used several times.
Figs come in three main varieties – red, white and black – and all three are suitable for cooking. They are sweet and juicy and complement well the stronger flavours of coffee and vanilla.

ingredients

1 **peach** or **nectarine**

75g/3oz/1 cup **crunchy toasted oat cereal**

150ml/¼ pint/⅔ cup **natural** (plain) **yogurt**

15ml/1 tbsp **pure fruit jam**

15ml/1 tbsp freshly squeezed **fruit juice**

cook's tips

If you prefer to use a flavoured toasted oat cereal (raisin and almond, perhaps, or tropical fruits) be sure to check the nutritional information on the label and choose the variety with the lowest amount of added sugar.

Any fruit jam and juice, which complement each other and the peach or nectarine, can be used.

crunchy oat, fruit & yogurt layer

CHUNKS OF PEACH OR NECTARINE AND **CRUNCHY** CEREAL CONTRAST IN TEXTURE IN THIS **EASY** AND TASTY COMBINATION.

method

SERVES 2

1 Halve the peach or nectarine, twist the two halves in opposite directions to separate and prise out the stone (pit). Cut the fruit into bitesize pieces with a sharp knife.

2 Divide the chopped peach or nectarine between 2 tall glasses, reserving a few pieces for decoration.

3 Sprinkle the toasted oat cereal over the fruit in an even layer, then top with the natural yogurt.

4 Stir the jam and fruit juice together, then drizzle the mixture over the yogurt. Decorate with the reserved peach or nectarine and serve immediately.

cheese & banana toasties

WHOLEMEAL TOAST TOPPED WITH **SOFT CHEESE** AND SLICED BANANA MAKES THE PERFECT BREAKFAST AND IS ESPECIALLY DELICIOUS WHEN DRIZZLED WITH **HONEY** AND GRILLED. IT'S QUICK AND EASY TO MAKE, AND PROVIDES A **DELICIOUS** START TO ANY DAY.

ingredients

4 thick slices of **wholemeal** (whole-wheat) **bread**

115g/4oz/½ cup **soft white** (farmer's) **cheese**

1.5ml/¼ tsp **cardamom seeds**, crushed (optional)

4 small **bananas**, peeled

20ml/4 tsp **clear honey**

variation

For a delicious variation, use fruited, sesame seed or caraway seed bread. Omit the cardamom seeds and sprinkle ground cinnamon on the bananas before adding the honey.

method

SERVES 4

1 Place the slices of bread on a rack in a grill (broiler) pan and toast on one side only until golden brown.

2 Turn the bread over and spread the untoasted side of each slice with soft cheese. Sprinkle over the crushed cardamom seeds, if using.

3 Slice the bananas and arrange the slices on top of the cheese, then drizzle each slice with 5ml/1 tsp of the clear honey.

4 Slide the pan back under the medium-hot grill and cook for a few minutes until bubbling. Serve immediately.

ingredients

1 large **pineapple**

1 large **mango**

25g/1oz/2 tbsp **unsalted** (sweet) **butter**, melted

4 thick slices **panettone**

For the vanilla yogurt

250g/9oz/generous 1 cup **Greek** (US strained plain) **yogurt**

30ml/2 tbsp **clear honey**

2.5ml/½ tsp **ground cinnamon**

a few drops **vanilla essence** (extract)

variation

Peaches and plums make a delicious alternative to these tropical fruits. Place 3 peaches in a bowl of boiling water for about 30 seconds. Remove with a slotted spoon and peel off the skin. Cut the flesh into slices, away from the stone. Slice 4 plums in the same way. Brush the slices of fruit with melted butter and cook as below.

mango & pineapple on panettone toast

GRIDDLING CONCENTRATES THE **SWEETNESS** OF BOTH THE PINEAPPLE AND MANGO, GIVING THEM A **CARAMEL** FLAVOUR THAT IS COMPLEMENTED BY THE **VANILLA YOGURT**.

method

SERVES 4

1 Cut the bottom and the spiky top off the pineapple, then stand it upright and cut off the skin, removing all the spikes, but as little of the flesh as possible. Lay the pineapple on its side and cut into quarters; remove the core if it is hard. Cut the pineapple into thick wedges.

2 To prepare the mango, cut away the 2 thick sides of the mango as close to the stone (pit) as possible. Peel the mango, then cut the remaining flesh from the stone. Slice the fruit and discard the stone.

3 Heat a griddle pan over a medium heat. Add the pineapple and mango (you may need to do this in batches). Brush with melted butter and cook for 8 minutes, turning once, until the fruit is soft and slightly golden. Alternatively, heat the grill (broiler) to high and line the rack with foil. Place the pineapple and mango on the foil, brush with butter and grill (broil) for 4 minutes on each side.

4 Meanwhile, place the yogurt in a bowl with the honey, cinnamon and vanilla and stir well.

5 Lightly toast the panettone, top with the grilled pineapple and mango and serve, accompanied by the vanilla yogurt.

fragrant fruit salad

THE SYRUP OF THIS **EXOTIC** FRUIT SALAD IS FLAVOURED AND SWEETENED WITH **LIME** AND **COFFEE LIQUEUR**. IT CAN BE PREPARED UP TO A DAY BEFORE SERVING.

method

SERVES 6

1 Put the sugar and lime rind in a small pan with 150ml/¼ pint/⅔ cup water. Heat gently until the sugar dissolves, then bring to the boil and simmer for 5 minutes. Remove the pan from the heat, leave to cool, then strain into a large serving bowl, discarding the lime rind. Stir in the lime juice and liqueur.

ingredients

130g/4½oz/⅔ cup **sugar**

thinly pared rind and juice of

   1 **lime**

60ml/4 tbsp coffee liqueur, such

   as **Tia Maria, Kahlúa** or

   Toussaint

1 small **pineapple**

1 **papaya**

2 **pomegranates**

1 **mango**

2 **passion fruits**

fine strips of **lime** peel,

   to decorate

> ### cook's tip
> To maximize the flavour of the fruit, leave the fruit salad to stand at room temperature for an hour before serving.

2 Using a sharp knife, cut the plume and stalk end from the pineapple. Peel thickly and cut the flesh into bitesize pieces, discarding the woody central core. Add to the bowl.

3 Cut the papaya in half and scoop out the seeds. Cut away the skin, then cut the fruit into slices. Cut the pomegranates in half and scoop out the seeds, discarding the membrane. Break into clusters and add to the bowl.

4 Cut the mango lengthways, along each side of the stone (pit). Peel the skin off the flesh. Add with the rest of the fruit to the bowl. Stir well.

5 Halve the passion fruits and scoop out the flesh using a teaspoon. Spoon over the salad, decorate with fine strips of lime peel and serve immediately.

caramelized apricots with pain perdu

PAIN PERDU IS A FRENCH INVENTION THAT LITERALLY TRANSLATES AS **"LOST BREAD"**. AMERICANS CALL IT **FRENCH TOAST**, WHILE A BRITISH VERSION IS KNOWN AS **POOR KNIGHTS**.

ingredients

75g/3oz/6 tbsp **unsalted** (sweet) **butter**, clarified

450g/1lb **apricots,** stoned (pitted) and thickly sliced

115g/4oz/generous ½ cup **caster** (superfine) **sugar**

150ml/¼ pint/⅔ cup **double** (heavy) **cream**

30ml/2 tbsp **apricot brandy or brandy**

For the pain perdu

600ml/1 pint/2½ cups **milk**

1 **vanilla pod** (bean)

50g/2oz/¼ cup **caster** (superfine) **sugar**

4 **large** (US extra large) **eggs**, beaten

115g/4oz/½ cup **unsalted** (sweet) **butter,** clarified

6 **brioche slices**, halved diagonally

2.5ml/½ tsp **ground cinnamon**

method

SERVES 6

1 Heat a heavy frying pan, then melt a quarter of the butter. Add the apricot slices and cook for 2–3 minutes until golden. Using a slotted spoon, transfer them to a bowl. Add the rest of the butter to the pan with the sugar and heat gently, stirring, until golden.

2 Pour in the cream and brandy and cook gently until the mixture forms a smooth sauce. Boil for 2–3 minutes until thickened, then pour the sauce over the apricots and set aside.

3 To make the pain perdu, pour the milk into a pan and add the vanilla pod and half the sugar. Heat gently until almost boiling, then remove the pan from the heat and set aside to cool.

4 Remove the vanilla pod and pour the flavoured milk into a shallow dish. Whisk in the eggs. Heat a sixth of the butter in the clean frying pan. Dip each slice of brioche in turn into the milk mixture, add it to the pan and fry until golden brown on both sides. Add the remaining butter as needed. As the pain perdu is cooked, remove the slices and keep hot.

5 Warm the apricot sauce and spoon it on to the pain perdu. Mix the remaining sugar with the ground cinnamon and sprinkle a little of the mixture over each portion.

---

cook's tips

To clarify the butter, melt it in a small pan, then leave it to stand for a few minutes. Carefully pour the clear butter on the surface (the clarified butter) into a small bowl, leaving the milky solids behind in the pan.

ingredients

300ml/½ pint/1¼ cups **red wine**

300ml/½ pint/1¼ cups **fresh orange juice**

finely grated rind and juice of 1 **orange**

45ml/3 tbsp **clear honey or barley malt syrup**

1 **cinnamon stick**, broken in half

4 **cloves**

4 **cardamom pods**, split

2 eating **pears**, peeled, cored and halved

8 ready-to-eat **dried figs**

12 ready-to-eat **dried apricots**

2 **eating apples**, peeled, cored and thickly sliced

winter fruit poached in mulled wine

FRESH **APPLES** AND **PEARS** ARE COMBINED WITH DRIED APRICOTS AND FIGS, AND COOKED IN A **FRAGRANT**, SPICY WINE UNTIL TENDER AND INTENSELY FLAVOURED.

method

SERVES 4

1 Put the wine, the fresh and squeezed orange juice and half the orange rind in a pan with the honey or syrup, cinnamon, cloves and split cardamom pods. Bring to the boil, then reduce the heat and simmer for 2 minutes, stirring occasionally.

2 Add the pears, figs and apricots to the pan and cook, covered, over a medium heat for 25 minutes, occasionally turning the fruit in the wine mixture. Add the sliced apples and cook for a further 12–15 minutes until all the fruit is tender.

3 Remove the fruit from the pan and discard the cinnamon, cloves and cardamom pods. Cook the wine mixture over a high heat until reduced and syrupy, then pour it over the fruit. Serve decorated with the reserved orange rind, if you like.

tropical fruit with rum & cinnamon

DARK RUM AND **CINNAMON** GIVE THIS HOT FRUIT SALAD A DISTINCTLY **CARIBBEAN FLAVOUR**. IT IS BEST EATEN AS SOON AS IT IS READY, SO PREPARE THE **FRUIT** AHEAD OF TIME, THEN COOK JUST BEFORE SERVING – THIS WILL ONLY TAKE A **FEW MINUTES**.

method

SERVES 4

1 Melt the butter in a large, heavy frying pan over a medium heat. Add the sliced pineapple and cook for 3 minutes, or until it starts to brown, turning it occasionally.

2 Add the prepared mango, papaya and bananas to the pan and cook for 1 minute, turning occasionally with a wooden spatula.

3 Add the honey or maple syrup, cinnamon and rum to the pan and stir gently to combine. Cook for a further 2 minutes or until the sauce thickens and the fruit is tender. Serve immediately with natural yogurt or yogurt ice.

variation
This can make a great dish for a family brunch as children always love the sweet and juicy pan-fried fruit. To make a child-friendly version, omit the rum and add 60ml/4 tbsp freshly squeezed orange juice instead.

ingredients

25g/1oz/2 tbsp **unsalted**
    (sweet) **butter**
1 **pineapple**, peeled, cored
    and sliced
1 **mango**, peeled, stoned (pitted)
    and cut into 1cm/½in cubes
1 **papaya**, peeled, halved,
    seeded and sliced
2 **bananas**, thickly sliced
30ml/2 tbsp **clear honey or
    maple syrup**
5ml/1 tsp **ground cinnamon**
60ml/4 tbsp **dark rum**
natural (plain) **yogurt** or **yogurt
    ice**, to serve

baking for breakfast

croissants

GOLDEN LAYERS OF FLAKY PASTRY – **PUFFY**, LIGHT AND FLAVOURED WITH **BUTTER** – IS HOW THE BEST CROISSANTS SHOULD BE. SERVE **WARM** WITH JAM AND BUTTER ON THE DAY OF **BAKING**.

ingredients

350g/12oz/3 cups **strong white** (bread) **flour**, plus extra for dusting
115g/4oz/1 cup fine **French plain** (all-purpose) **flour**
5ml/1 tsp **salt**
25g/1oz/2 tbsp **caster** (superfine) **sugar**
15g/½oz **fresh yeast**
200ml/7fl oz/scant 1 cup lukewarm **milk**
1 **egg**, lightly beaten
225g/8oz/1 cup **butter**

For the glaze
1 **egg yolk**
15ml/1 tbsp **milk**

---

cook's tip
Make sure that the block of butter and the dough are about the same temperature when combining, to ensure the best results.

---

variation
To make chocolate-filled croissants, place a small square of milk or plain (semisweet) chocolate or 15ml/ 1 tbsp coarsely chopped chocolate at the wide end of each triangle before rolling up as in step 6.

---

method

MAKES 14 CROISSANTS

1 Sift the flours and salt into a bowl. Stir in the sugar. Make a well in the centre. Cream the yeast with 45ml/3 tbsp of the milk, then stir in the remainder. Add the yeast mixture to the centre of the flour, then add the egg and gradually beat in the flour until it forms a dough.

2 Turn out on to a floured surface and knead for 3–4 minutes. Place in an oiled bowl, cover with oiled clear film (plastic wrap) and leave to rise in a warm place for 45 minutes–1 hour, or until doubled in bulk.

3 Knock back (punch down), re-cover and chill in the refrigerator for 1 hour. Meanwhile, flatten the butter into a 2cm/¾in thick block. Knock back the dough and turn out on to a floured surface. Roll out into a 25cm/10in square, rolling the edges thinner than the centre.

4 Place the butter diagonally in the centre and fold the corners of the dough over it like an envelope, tucking in the edges. Roll the dough into a rectangle 2cm/¾in thick, about twice as long as it is wide. Fold the bottom third up and the top third down and seal the edges with a rolling pin. Wrap in clear film and chill for 20 minutes.

5 Repeat the rolling, folding and chilling twice more, turning the dough by 90 degrees each time. Roll out on a floured surface into a 63 × 33cm/25 × 13in rectangle; trim to leave a 60 × 30cm/ 24 × 12in rectangle. Cut in half lengthwise. Cut crosswise into 14 equal triangles with 15cm/6in bases. Place the triangles on two baking sheets, cover with clear film and chill for 10 minutes.

6 To shape the croissants, place each with the wide end at the top, hold each side and pull gently to stretch the top, then roll towards the point, finishing with the pointed end underneath. Curve towards the pointed end to make a crescent. Space out on two baking sheets.

7 Combine the egg yolk and milk for the glaze. Lightly brush a little glaze over the croissants, avoiding the cut edges. Cover loosely with lightly oiled clear film and leave to rise in a warm place for about 30 minutes, or until they are nearly doubled in size.

8 Meanwhile, preheat the oven to 220°C/425°F/Gas 7. Brush the croissants with the remaining glaze and bake for 15–20 minutes, or until crisp and golden. Transfer to a wire rack to cool slightly.

ingredients

450g/1lb/4 cups **plain**
 (all-purpose) **white flour**,
 plus extra for dusting
10ml/2 tsp **salt**
20g/¾oz **fresh yeast**
150ml/¼ pint/⅔ cup
 lukewarm **milk**
150ml/¼ pint/⅔ cup lukewarm
 water
30ml/2 tbsp **milk**, for glazing

scottish morning rolls

THESE LIGHT, WHITE ROLLS ARE **BEST**
SERVED **WARM**, AS SOON AS THEY ARE
BAKED. IN SCOTLAND THEY ARE A FIRM
BREAKFAST FAVOURITE, SERVED WITH
A FRIED EGG AND BACON.

method

MAKES 10

1 Grease 2 baking sheets. Sift the flour and salt together into a large
bowl and make a well in the centre. Mix the yeast with the milk, then
mix in the water. Add to the centre of the flour and mix together to
form a soft dough.

2 Knead the dough lightly in the bowl, then cover with lightly oiled clear
film (plastic wrap) and leave to rise, in a warm place, for 1 hour, or
until doubled in bulk. Turn the dough out on to a lightly floured surface
and knock back (punch down).

3 Divide the dough into 10 equal pieces. Knead lightly and, using a
rolling pin, shape each piece to a flat oval 10 × 7.5cm/4 × 3in or
a flat round 9cm/3½in.

4 Transfer to the baking sheets, spaced well apart, and cover with oiled
clear film. Leave to rise, in a warm place, for about 30 minutes.

5 Meanwhile, preheat the oven to 200°C/400°F/Gas 6. Press each roll
in the centre with the three middle fingers to equalize the air bubbles
and to help prevent blistering. Brush with milk and dust with flour.
Bake for 15–20 minutes or until lightly browned. Dust with more flour
and cool slightly on a wire rack. Serve warm.

sweet potato & honey bread rolls

THESE **WONDERFUL,** SLIGHTLY **SWEET** ROLLS TASTE JUST AS **DELICIOUS** SERVED WITH **FRUIT** CONSERVES OR HONEY AS WITH A WHOLESOME **SAVOURY SOUP**.

method

MAKES 12

1 Cook the sweet potato in a large pan of boiling water for 45 minutes, or until very tender.

2 Meanwhile, sift the flour into a large mixing bowl, add the dried yeast, ground nutmeg and cumin seeds and give the ingredients a good stir to combine well.

3 In a jug (pitcher), mix together the honey and milk. Drain the potato and peel the skin. Mash the potato flesh and add to the flour mixture with the liquid.

4 Combine the potato and flour mixture and bring together into a ball. Knead the dough for about 5 minutes on a floured surface. Place the dough in a bowl and cover with a damp cloth. Leave to rise in a warm place for about 30 minutes.

5 Turn the dough out and knock back (punch down) to remove any air bubbles. Divide the dough into 12 pieces and shape each piece into a round.

6 Lightly grease a baking sheet. Place the rolls on the prepared baking sheet. Cover with a damp cloth and leave to rise for 30 minutes, or until doubled in size. Preheat the oven to 220°C/425°F/Gas 7.

7 Bake for 10 minutes. Remove from the oven and drizzle with more honey and sprinkle with more cumin seeds before serving.

ingredients

1 large **sweet potato**

225g/8oz/2 cups **strong white** (bread) **flour**, plus extra for dusting

5ml/1 tsp **easy-blend** (rapid-rise) **dried yeast**

pinch of **ground nutmeg**

pinch of **cumin seeds**, plus extra for sprinkling

5ml/1 tsp clear **honey**, plus extra for drizzling

200ml/7fl oz/scant 1 cup lukewarm **milk**

oil, for greasing

cook's tip
This dough is quite sticky, so handle with care and use plenty of flour on your hands and the surface when you are kneading and rolling it.

crumpets

HOME-MADE CRUMPETS ARE **LESS DOUGHY** AND NOT AS HEAVY AS MOST SUPERMARKET VERSIONS. SERVE THEM LIGHTLY TOASTED, **OOZING** WITH **BUTTER**.

ingredients

oil, for greasing

225g/8oz/2 cups **plain** (all-purpose) **flour**

225g/8oz/2 cups **strong white** (bread) **flour**

10ml/2 tsp **salt**

600ml/1 pint/2½ cups **milk** and **water** mixed

30ml/2 tbsp **sunflower oil**

15ml/1 tbsp **caster** (superfine) **sugar**

15g/½oz **fresh yeast**

2.5ml/½ tsp **bicarbonate of soda** (baking soda)

120ml/4fl oz/½ cup lukewarm **water**

cook's tip

If the characteristic bubbles do not form on the crumpets as they cook, add a little more water to the batter before cooking the next batch of crumpets.

method

MAKES ABOUT 20

1 Lightly grease a griddle or heavy frying pan and 4 × 8cm/1½ × 3¼in plain pastry cutters or crumpet rings.

2 Sift the flours and salt together into a large bowl and make a well in the centre. Heat the milk and water mixture, oil and sugar until lukewarm. Mix the yeast with 150ml/¼ pint/⅔ cup of this liquid.

3 Add the yeast mixture and remaining liquid to the centre of the flour and beat vigorously for about 5 minutes until smooth and elastic. Cover with lightly oiled clear film (plastic wrap) and leave to rise in a warm place for about 1½ hours, or until the mixture is bubbly.

4 Dissolve the soda in the lukewarm water and stir into the batter. Recover and leave to rise for 30 minutes.

5 Place the cutters or crumpet rings on the griddle and warm over a medium heat. Fill the cutters or rings a generous 1cm/½in deep. Cook over a gentle heat for 6–7 minutes. The tops should be dry, with a mass of tiny holes. Remove the cutters or rings and turn the crumpets over. Cook for 1–2 minutes or until pale golden. Repeat with remaining batter. Serve warm.

english muffins

PERFECT SERVED WARM, SPLIT OPEN WITH **BUTTER** AND JAM OR TRY THESE FAVOURITES **TOASTED**, SPLIT AND TOPPED WITH **HAM AND EGGS** FOR BRUNCH.

cook's tip

Muffins should be cut around the outer edge only using a sharp knife and then torn apart. If toasting, toast the whole muffins first and then split them in half.
If you'd like to serve the muffins warm, transfer them to a wire rack to cool slightly before serving.

ingredients

450g/1lb/4 cups **strong white** (bread) **flour**, plus extra for dusting

oil, for greasing

7.5ml/1½ tsp **salt**

350–375ml/12–13fl oz/ 1½–1⅔ cups lukewarm **milk**

2.5ml/½ tsp **caster** (superfine) **sugar**

15g/½oz **fresh yeast**

15ml/1 tbsp **melted butter** or **olive oil**

rice flour or **semolina**, for dusting

method

MAKES 9

1 Generously flour a non-stick baking sheet. Very lightly grease a griddle. Sift the flour and salt together into a large bowl and make a well in the centre. Blend 150ml/¼ pint/⅔ cup of the milk, sugar and yeast together. Stir in the remaining milk and butter or olive oil.

2 Add the yeast mixture to the well and beat for 4–5 minutes until smooth and elastic. The dough will be soft, but just hold its shape. Cover with lightly oiled clear film (plastic wrap) and leave to rise in a warm place for 45–60 minutes, or until doubled in bulk.

3 Turn out the dough on a well-floured surface and knock back (punch down). Roll out to about 1cm/½in thick. Using a floured 7.5cm/3in plain cutter, cut out 9 rounds.

4 Dust with rice flour or semolina and place on the prepared baking sheet. Cover and leave to rise in a warm place for 20–30 minutes.

5 Warm the griddle over a medium heat. Carefully transfer the muffins in batches to the griddle. Cook slowly for about 7 minutes on each side or until golden brown. Transfer to a wire rack to cool. Serve warm.

ingredients

oil, for greasing

350g/12oz/3 cups **strong white**
    (bread) **flour**, plus extra
    for dusting

10ml/2 tsp **salt**

6g/¼oz sachet **easy-blend**
    (rapid-rise) **dried yeast**

5ml/1 tsp **malt extract**

210ml/7½fl oz/scant 1 cup
    lukewarm **water**

For poaching

2.5 litres/4 pints/10¼ cups
    water

15ml/1 tbsp **malt extract**

For the topping

1 **egg white**

10ml/2 tsp cold **water**

30ml/2 tbsp **poppy, sesame** or
    caraway seeds

bagels

BAGELS ARE THE TRADITIONAL **JEWISH** ROLL
WITH A HOLE. THEY HAVE A WONDERFUL,
CHEWY TEXTURE, ACHIEVED BY **POACHING**
THE DOUGH BEFORE COOKING. THEY ARE
DELICIOUS **TOASTED** OR FILLED. FOR A
REALLY DECADENT BRUNCH, **GENEROUSLY
FILL** FRESH BAGELS WITH CREAM CHEESE
AND **SMOKED SALMON**.

method

MAKES 10 BAGELS

1 Grease 2 baking sheets. Sift the flour and salt together into a large
bowl. Stir in the dried yeast. Make a well in the centre. Mix the malt
extract and water, add to the centre of the flour and mix to a dough.
Knead on a floured surface until elastic.

2 Place in an oiled bowl, cover with oiled clear film (plastic wrap) and
leave to rise in a warm place for 1 hour, or until doubled in bulk.

3 Turn out the dough on to a lightly floured surface and knock back
(punch down). Knead for 1 minute, then divide into 10 equal pieces.
Shape into balls, cover with clear film and leave to rest for 5 minutes.

4 Gently flatten each ball and make a hole through the centre with your
thumb. Enlarge the hole slightly by turning your thumb around. Place
on a floured tray, re-cover and leave in a warm place for about
10–20 minutes, or until they begin to rise.

5 Meanwhile, preheat the oven to 220ºC/425ºF/Gas 7. Place the water
and malt extract for poaching in a large pan, bring to the boil, then
reduce to a simmer. Place the bagels in the water 2 or 3 at a time
and poach for about 1 minute. They will sink and then rise again when
first added to the pan. Using a fish slice (metal spatula) or large
draining spoon, turn over and cook for 30 seconds. Remove and drain
on a dishtowel. Repeat with the remaining bagels.

6 Place 5 bagels on each prepared baking sheet, spacing them well
apart. Beat the egg white with the water for the topping, brush the
mixture over the top of each bagel and sprinkle with poppy, sesame or
caraway seeds. Bake for 20–25 minutes, or until golden brown.
Transfer to a wire rack to cool.

blueberry muffins

THESE **LIGHT** AND **FRUITY** MUFFINS ARE DELICIOUS SERVED WARM, **STRAIGHT FROM THE OVEN** FOR BREAKFAST OR BRUNCH.

method

MAKES 12

1 Preheat the oven to 200°C/400°F/Gas 6. Grease a 12 cup muffin tin (pan) or arrange 12 paper muffin cases on a baking tray.

2 Sift together the flour, sugar, baking powder and salt into a large mixing bowl. In another bowl, whisk the eggs until blended.

3 Add the melted butter, milk, vanilla and lemon rind to the eggs, and stir thoroughly to combine.

4 Make a well in the dry ingredients and pour in the egg mixture. With a large metal spoon, stir gently until the flour is just moistened, but not completely smooth. Add the blueberries to the muffin mixture and gently fold in, being careful not to crush the berries.

5 Spoon the batter into the muffin tin or paper cases, leaving enough room for the muffins to rise.

6 Bake for 20–25 minutes, until the tops spring back when touched lightly. Leave the muffins in the tin, if using, for 5 minutes before turning out on to a wire rack to cool a little before serving. Transfer muffins baked in paper cases to the wire rack to cool slightly before serving.

ingredients

180g/6¼oz/generous 1½ cups
   plain (all-purpose) **flour**
60g/2¼oz/generous ¼ cup
   caster (superfine) **sugar**
10ml/2 tsp **baking powder**
   (baking soda)
1.5ml/¼ tsp **salt**
2 **eggs**
50g/2oz/¼ cup **butter**, melted
175ml/6fl oz/¾ cup **milk**
5ml/1 tsp **vanilla**
   essence (extract)
5ml/1 tsp **grated lemon rind**
175g/6oz/1½ cups
   fresh blueberries

variation
Muffins are delicious with all kinds of different fruits. Try out some variations using this basic muffin recipe. Replace the blueberries with the same weight of bilberries, blackcurrants, pitted cherries or raspberries.

egg dishes

sweet persian breakfast omelette

THIS **SIMPLE**, LIGHT AND **FLUFFY** OMELETTE IS POPULAR THROUGHOUT THE MIDDLE EAST AND IS VERY GOOD EATEN WITH A **FRUITY** HOME-MADE JAM OR **CONSERVE**. IT MAKES AN **EXCELLENT** LIGHT BRUNCH DISH.

ingredients

3 **eggs**

10ml/2 tsp **caster**
(superfine) **sugar**

5ml/1 tsp **plain**
(all-purpose) **flour**

10g/¼oz/½ tbsp **unsalted**
(sweet) **butter**

bread and **jam**, to serve

method

SERVES 1

1 Break the eggs into a large bowl, add the sugar and flour and beat until really frothy. Heat the butter in an omelette pan until it begins to bubble, then pour in the egg mixture and cook, without stirring, until it begins to set.

2 Run a wooden spatula around the edge of the omelette, then carefully turn it over and cook the second side for 1–2 minutes until golden. Serve hot or warm with thick slices of fresh bread and fruity jam.

cook's tip
Continue the Middle Eastern theme when choosing a jam to serve with this omelette. Pick a conserve made from fruits such as fig or apricot that are popular in the Middle East. Alternatively, use raspberry or strawberry jam, which will be just as good and are always popular with children.

chive scrambled eggs in brioches

SCRAMBLED EGGS ARE DELICIOUS AT **ANY TIME** OF DAY BUT, WHEN SERVED WITH **FRANCE'S FAVOURITE** BREAKFAST BREAD, THEY BECOME THE **ULTIMATE** BREAKFAST OR BRUNCH **TREAT**. THESE SCRAMBLED EGGS ARE SOFTER AND CREAMIER THAN OTHER VERSIONS, AND TASTE GOOD **SERVED COLD**

ingredients

4 individual **brioches**

6 **eggs,** beaten

30ml/2 tbsp chopped **fresh**
chives, plus extra to garnish

25g/1oz/2 tbsp **unsalted**
(sweet) **butter**

45ml/3 tbsp **cottage cheese**

60–75ml/4–5 tbsp **double**
(heavy) **cream**

salt and **ground black pepper**

method

SERVES 4

1 Preheat the oven to 180°C/350°F/Gas 4. Cut the tops off the brioches and set aside. Carefully scoop out the centre of each brioche, leaving a bread shell. Put the brioche shells and lids on a baking sheet and bake for 5 minutes until hot and crisp.

2 Lightly beat the eggs and season to taste. Add about half the chives. Heat the butter in a medium pan until it begins to foam, then add the eggs and cook, stirring with a wooden spoon until semi-solid.

3 Stir in the cottage cheese, cream and the rest of the chives and continue to cook for 1–2 minutes, making sure that the eggs remain soft and creamy.

4 To serve, spoon the eggs into the crisp brioche shells and sprinkle with the extra chives.

cook's tip
Save the scooped-out brioche centres and freeze them in an airtight container. Partly thaw and blend or grate them to make crumbs for coating fish or pieces of chicken before frying.

ingredients

4 **eggs**

2 **English muffins** or 4 slices
    of **bread**

butter, for spreading

4 thick **cooked ham** slices, cut
    to fit the muffins

fresh chives, to garnish

For the sauce

3 **egg yolks**

30ml/2 tbsp **fresh lemon juice**

1.5ml/¼ tsp **salt**

115g/4oz/½ cup **butter**

30ml/2 tbsp **single** (light) **cream**

ground black pepper

> ### cook's tip
> Use only very fresh eggs for
> poaching, because they keep their
> shape better in the water.

eggs benedict

THIS **DELICIOUS** BRUNCH DISH IS THOUGHT
TO HAVE BEEN CREATED AT **DELMONICO'S
RESTAURANT** IN NEW YORK FOR MR AND
MRS LEGRAND BENEDICT. THE COMBINATION
OF **SMOKY HAM**, LIGHTLY **POACHED EGGS**
AND A CREAMY, **LEMON** SAUCE IS PERFECT.

method   SERVES 4

1 To make the sauce, blend the egg yolks, lemon juice and salt in a
   food processor or blender for 15 seconds. Melt the butter in a small
   pan until it bubbles, but do not let it brown.

2 With the motor running, slowly pour the hot butter into the food
   processor or blender through the feeder tube in a slow, steady stream.
   Turn off the machine as soon as all the butter has been added.

3 Pour the sauce into a bowl, placed over a pan of simmering water. Stir
   for 2–3 minutes, until thickened. If the sauce begins to curdle, whisk
   in 15ml/1 tbsp boiling water. Stir in the cream and season with
   pepper. Remove from the heat and keep warm over the pan.

4 Bring a shallow pan of lightly salted water to the boil. Break each
   egg into a cup, then slide it carefully into the water. Delicately turn
   the white around the yolk with a spoon. Cook for 3–4 minutes
   until the white is set.

5 Remove the eggs from the pan, 1 at a time, using a slotted spoon,
   and drain on kitchen paper. Cut off any ragged edges with a small
   knife or scissors.

6 While the eggs are poaching, split and toast the muffins or toast the
   slices of bread. Spread with butter while still warm.

7 Place a piece of ham, which you may brown in butter if you like, on
   each muffin half or slice of toast, then place an egg on each ham-
   topped muffin. Spoon the warm sauce over the eggs, garnish with
   chives and serve.

poached eggs florentine

THIS **CLASSIC COMBINATION** OF POACHED EGGS, LIGHTLY SAUTEED **SPINACH** AND A CREAMY **CHEESE SAUCE** WILL ALWAYS MAKE AN UNBEATABLE BRUNCH DISH.

method

SERVES 4

1 Preheat the oven to 200°C/400°F/Gas 6. Place the spinach in a large pan with a very small amount of water. Cook for 3–4 minutes, then drain well and chop finely.

2 Return the spinach to the pan, add the butter, cream, nutmeg and seasoning, and heat through. Spoon into 4 small gratin dishes, making a well in the middle of each.

3 To make the topping, heat the butter in a small pan, add the flour and cook over a low heat for 1 minute, stirring constantly. Gradually blend in the hot milk, beating well.

4 Cook for 2 minutes, stirring constantly. Remove from the heat and stir in the mace and 75g/3oz/¾ cup of the Gruyère cheese.

5 Break each egg into a cup and slide it into a pan of lightly salted simmering water. Poach for 3–4 minutes. Lift out the eggs and drain. Place a poached egg in the middle of each dish and cover with the cheese sauce. Sprinkle with the remaining cheeses and bake for 10 minutes or until just golden. Serve with Parmesan shavings.

ingredients

675g/1½lb **spinach**, washed and
  drained
25g/1oz/2 tbsp **butter**
60ml/4 tbsp **double**
  (heavy) **cream**
pinch of freshly grated **nutmeg**
salt and **ground black pepper**

For the topping
25g/1oz/2 tbsp **butter**
25g/1oz/¼ cup **plain**
  (all-purpose) **flour**
300ml/½ pint/1¼ cups hot **milk**
pinch of ground **mace**
115g/4oz/1 cup grated
  Gruyère cheese
4 **eggs**
15ml/1 tbsp freshly grated
  Parmesan cheese, plus fresh
  Parmesan shavings to serve

cook's tip
This dish can be prepared with any other green vegetable that is in season, such as chard, fennel or Chinese leaves (Chinese cabbage).

ingredients

175g/6oz **smoked haddock**
fillet, poached and drained

50g/2oz/¼ cup **butter**, diced

175ml/6fl oz/¾ cup **whipping** or
double (heavy) **cream**

4 **eggs**, separated

40g/1½oz/⅓ cup grated mature
(sharp) **Cheddar cheese**

ground black pepper

watercress, to garnish

cook's tip

Try to buy smoked haddock that does
not contain artificial colouring for this
recipe. Besides being better for you,
it gives the omelette a lighter, more
attractive colour.

omelette arnold · bennett

THIS CREAMY, SMOKED HADDOCK **SOUFFLÉ OMELETTE** VIRTUALLY MELTS IN THE MOUTH. MILD, CREAMY EGGS **COMPLEMENT** THE PUNGENT, SMOKY FISH PERFECTLY.

method

SERVES 2

1 Remove the skin and any bones from the haddock fillet and discard. Carefully flake the flesh using a fork.

2 Melt half the butter with 60ml/4 tbsp of the cream in a fairly small non-stick pan, then add the flaked fish and stir together gently. Cover the pan with a lid, remove from the heat and set aside to cool.

3 Mix the egg yolks with 15ml/1 tbsp of the cream. Season with pepper, then stir into the fish. In a separate bowl, mix the cheese and the remaining cream. Stiffly whisk the egg whites, then fold into the fish mixture. Heat the remaining butter in an omelette pan, add the fish mixture and cook until browned underneath. Pour the cheese mixture over and grill (broil) until bubbling. Garnish with watercress and serve.

soufflé omelette with mushrooms

THIS LIGHT SOUFFLÉ OMELETTE MAKES AN **IDEAL VEGETARIAN** BRUNCH OMELETTE. USE A COMBINATION OF **DIFFERENT** WILD AND CULTIVATED **MUSHROOMS**, SUCH AS OYSTER OR CHESTNUT, IF YOU LIKE.

method

SERVES 1

1 To make the mushroom sauce, melt the butter in a small pan and add the sliced mushrooms. Fry gently for 4–5 minutes, stirring occasionally, until tender.

2 Stir in the flour, then gradually add the milk, stirring constantly. Cook until boiling and thickened. Add the parsley, if using, and season with salt and pepper. Keep warm.

3 Beat the egg yolks in a large bowl with 15ml/1 tbsp water and season with a little salt and pepper. Whisk the egg whites in a separate bowl until stiff, then fold into the egg yolks using a metal spoon. Preheat the grill (broiler).

4 Melt the butter in a large frying pan and pour the egg mixture into the pan. Cook over a gentle heat for 2–4 minutes. Place the frying pan under the grill and cook for a further 3–4 minutes until the top is golden brown.

5 Slide the omelette on to a warmed serving plate, pour the mushroom sauce over the top and fold the omelette in half. Serve, garnished with parsley or coriander leaves.

ingredients

2 **eggs**, separated
15g/½oz/1 tbsp **butter**
flat leaf **parsley** or **coriander** (cilantro) leaves, to garnish

For the mushroom sauce
15g/½oz/1 tbsp **butter**
75g/3oz/generous 1 cup **button** (white) **mushrooms,** thinly sliced
15ml/1 tbsp **plain** (all-purpose) **flour**
75–120ml/3–4fl oz/ ⅓–½ cup **milk**
5ml/1 tsp chopped **fresh parsley** (optional)
salt and **ground black pepper**

cook's tip
For extra flavour, add a splash of mushroom ketchup or a few drops of Tabasco sauce to the mushrooms as they cook.

muffins with bacon & eggs

THIS MAKES A TERRIFIC **CELEBRATION BREAKFAST**, IDEAL FOR BIRTHDAYS, ANNIVERSARIES OR OTHER DAYS WHEN YOU WANT TO SET OUT WITH A **SMILE** ON YOUR FACE. YOU WILL NEED A FOOD PROCESSOR OR BLENDER TO MAKE THE **SPEEDY** VERSION OF **HOLLANDAISE** SAUCE.

ingredients

method

SERVES 4

350g/12oz **rindless back** (lean) **bacon** rashers (strips)

dash of **white wine vinegar**

4 **eggs**

4 **English muffins**

butter, for spreading

For the hollandaise sauce

2 **egg yolks**

5ml/1 tsp **white wine vinegar**

75g/3oz/6 tbsp **butter**

salt and **ground black pepper**

1 Preheat the grill (broiler) and cook the bacon for 5–8 minutes, turning once, or until crisp and brown on both sides.

2 Fill a large frying pan with water and bring to the boil. Add the vinegar and regulate the heat so that the water is gently simmering. Crack the eggs into the water and poach them for 3–4 minutes, or slightly longer for firm eggs.

3 Split and toast the muffins while the eggs are cooking. Spread with butter and place on warmed plates.

4 To make the hollandaise sauce, process the egg yolks and white wine vinegar in a blender or food processor. Melt the butter. With the motor still running, very gradually add the hot melted butter through the feeder tube. The hot butter cooks the yolks to make a thick, glossy sauce. Switch off the machine as soon as all the butter has been added and the sauce has thickened. Season to taste.

5 Arrange the bacon on the muffins and add a poached egg to each. Top with a spoonful of sauce and grind over some black pepper. Serve immediately.

cook's tip

Eggs that are 1 week or more old will not keep their shape when poached so, for the best results, use very fresh free-range organic eggs. To make sure that you don't break the yolk, crack the eggs into a cup before carefully adding them to the gently simmering water.

ingredients

2 slices **bread**

40g/1½oz/3 tbsp **butter**, plus
  extra for spreading

anchovy paste, such as
  Gentleman's Relish,
  for spreading

2 **eggs** and 2 **egg yolks**, beaten

60–90ml/4–6 tbsp **single** (light)
  cream or milk

salt and **ground black pepper**

anchovy fillets, cut into strips,
  and **paprika**, to garnish

savoury scrambled eggs

THESE **CREAMY** SCRAMBLED EGGS MAKE A
GREAT BRUNCH DISH. THE ADDITION OF
ANCHOVY GIVES THE MILD EGGS A SUBTLE
KICK. SERVE WITH A GLASS OF **CRISP
WHITE WINE** AND FOLLOW WITH A CHILLED,
FRESH FRUIT SALAD.

method

SERVES 2

1 Toast the bread, spread with butter and anchovy paste, then remove
   the crusts and cut into triangles. Keep warm.

2 Melt the rest of the butter in a medium non-stick pan, then stir in the
   beaten eggs, cream or milk, and a little salt and pepper. Heat very
   gently, stirring constantly, until the mixture begins to thicken.

3 Remove the pan from the heat and continue to stir until the mixture
   becomes very creamy, but do not allow it to harden.

4 Divide the scrambled eggs among the triangles of toast and garnish
   each with strips of anchovy fillet and a generous sprinkling of paprika.
   Serve immediately, while still hot.

pipérade with crostini

THIS MIXTURE OF SWEET PEPPERS, **TOMATOES** AND EGGS HAS ALL THE FLAVOURS OF THE **MEDITERRANEAN**. IT IS PERFECT FOR A LAZY WEEKEND BRUNCH.

method

MAKES 12

1 Heat the fat or oil in a large, heavy frying pan. Add the onions and cook over a gentle heat, stirring occasionally, for about 5 minutes until softened, but not coloured.

2 Add the peppers, garlic and chilli powder or cayenne. Cook for a further 5 minutes stirring, then add the plum tomatoes, oregano and seasoning and cook over a medium heat for 15–20 minutes until the peppers are soft and most of the liquid has evaporated.

3 Preheat the oven to 200°C/400°F/Gas 6. Cut the bread in half lengthways, trim off the ends, then cut into 6 equal pieces and brush with the extra virgin olive oil. Place on baking trays and bake for 8–10 minutes until crisp and just turning golden.

4 Heat the butter in a non-stick pan until it bubbles, add the eggs and stir until softly scrambled. Turn off the heat and stir in the pepper mixture. Divide evenly among the pieces of bread and sprinkle with the basil leaves. Serve hot or warm.

ingredients

60ml/4 tbsp **bacon fat, duck fat** or **olive oil**

2 small **onions**, coarsely chopped

4 **red, orange** or **yellow (bell) peppers**, seeded and chopped

2 large **garlic cloves**, finely chopped

pinch of **chilli** or **hot cayenne pepper**

675g/1½lb ripe **plum tomatoes**, peeled, seeded and chopped

15ml/1 tbsp chopped **fresh oregano** or 5ml/1 tsp dried

1 long **French stick**

60–90ml/4–6 tbsp **extra virgin olive oil**

25g/1oz/2 tbsp **butter**

6 **eggs**, beaten

salt and **ground black pepper**

fresh basil leaves, to garnish

cook's tip
To make a quick version for a crowd, cut the bread into thick slices before baking as above. Heat 200ml/7fl oz/ scant 1 cup ready-made sweet (bell) pepper and tomato pasta sauce until hot and add to the eggs in step 4.

ingredients

75ml/5 tbsp **olive oil**

175g/6oz **chorizo** or **spicy sausages,** thinly sliced

675g/1½lb **potatoes**, peeled and thinly sliced

275g/10oz **onions**, halved and thinly sliced

4 **eggs**, beaten

30ml/2 tbsp chopped **fresh parsley,** plus extra to garnish

115g/4oz/1 cup grated **Cheddar cheese**

salt and **ground black pepper**

spicy sausage & cheese tortilla

A **COLOURFUL**, SPANISH-STYLE OMELETTE, WHICH IS DELICIOUS **HOT OR COLD**. CUT INTO WEDGES TO SERVE.

method

SERVES 4–6

1 Heat 15ml/1 tbsp of the oil in a non-stick frying pan, about 20cm/8in in diameter, and fry the sausage until golden brown and cooked through. Lift out with a slotted spoon and drain on kitchen paper.

2 Add a further 30ml/2 tbsp oil to the pan and add the potatoes and onions (the pan will be very full).

3 Cook the potatoes and onions for 2–3 minutes, turning them frequently, then cover the pan tightly and cook over a gentle heat for about 30 minutes, turning the vegetables occasionally, until softened and slightly golden.

4 In a mixing bowl, mix the beaten eggs with the parsley, cheese, sausage and plenty of seasoning. Gently stir in the potatoes and onions, taking care not to break up the potato slices too much.

5 Wipe out the pan with kitchen paper and heat the remaining 30ml/2 tbsp oil. Add the potato mixture and cook over a very low heat, until the egg begins to set. Use a palette knife (spatula) to prevent the tortilla from sticking to the sides.

6 Preheat the grill (broiler) to hot. When the base of the tortilla has set, which should take about 5 minutes, protect the pan handle with foil and place under the grill until the tortilla is set and golden. Cut into wedges and scatter over some chopped parsley to garnish.

goat's cheese soufflé

MAKE SURE EVERYONE IS **SEATED** BEFORE THIS SOUFFLÉ IS **SERVED** BECAUSE IT WILL BEGIN TO DEFLATE ALMOST IMMEDIATELY. THE PUNGENT FLAVOUR OF GOAT'S CHEESE GIVES THIS **AIRY** SOUFFLÉ A REAL **BITE**.

method

SERVES 4

1 Melt the butter in a heavy pan over a medium heat. Stir in the flour and cook until slightly golden, stirring occasionally. Pour in half the milk, stir until smooth, then add the remaining milk and the bay leaf. Season with salt and plenty of ground black pepper and nutmeg. Reduce the heat to medium-low, cover and simmer gently for about 5 minutes, stirring occasionally.

2 Preheat the oven to 190°C/375°F/Gas 5. Butter a 1.5 litre/2½ pint/6¼ cup soufflé dish and sprinkle with Parmesan cheese. Remove the sauce from the heat and discard the bay leaf. Stir in the other cheeses.

3 In a large bowl, using a balloon whisk or electric mixer, whisk the egg whites slowly until they become frothy. Add the cream of tartar, increase the speed and continue whisking until they form stiff peaks that just flop over a little at the top.

4 Stir a spoonful of the beaten egg whites into the cheese sauce to lighten it, then pour the cheese sauce over the rest of the whites. Using a rubber spatula or large metal spoon, gently fold the sauce into the egg whites, cutting down through the centre to the bottom, then along the side of the bowl and up to the top, until the cheese sauce and egg whites are just combined.

5 Gently pour the soufflé mixture into the prepared dish and bake for about 30 minutes until puffed and golden brown. Serve immediately.

ingredients

25g/1oz/2 tbsp **butter**; plus extra for greasing

25g/1oz/2 tbsp **plain (all-purpose) flour**

175ml/6fl oz/¾ cup **milk**

1 **bay leaf**

freshly grated **nutmeg**

freshly grated **Parmesan cheese**, for sprinkling

40g/1½oz **herb and garlic soft (farmer's) cheese**

150g/5oz/1¼ cups **firm goat's cheese**, diced

6 **egg whites**, at room temperature

1.5ml/¼ tsp **cream of tartar**

salt and **ground black pepper**

variation
Use a blue cheese, such as Roquefort or Stilton, instead of goat's cheese.

twice-baked soufflés

THESE LITTLE SOUFFLÉS ARE SERVED **UPSIDE-DOWN**. THEY ARE REMARKABLY SIMPLE TO MAKE AND CAN BE PREPARED UP TO A **DAY IN ADVANCE** FOR AN EASY, **STRESS-FREE** BRUNCH.

ingredients

20g/¾oz/1½ tbsp **butter**, plus
  extra for greasing
30ml/2 tbsp **plain**
  (all-purpose) **flour**
150ml/¼ pint/⅔ cup **milk**
1 small **bay leaf**
2 **eggs**, separated, plus 1 **egg**
  white, at room temperature
115g/4oz/1 cup grated
  Gruyère cheese
1.5ml/¼ tsp **cream of tartar**
250ml/8fl oz/1 cup **double**
  (heavy) **cream**
25g/1oz/¼ cup **flaked**
  (sliced) **almonds**
salt, ground black pepper and
  grated nutmeg
sprigs of **fresh parsley**,
  to garnish

cook's tip
If you are making these soufflés in advance, cool the once-cooked soufflés, then cover and chill. It is important to bring the soufflés back to room temperature before baking, so remove them from the refrigerator in plenty of time.

variation
Other strongly flavoured cheeses could be used. Try mature (sharp) Cheddar, blue Stilton or Emmenthal.

method

SERVES 6

1 Preheat the oven to 190°C/375°F/Gas 5. Lightly grease six 175ml/ 6fl oz/¾ cup ramekins, then line the bases with buttered greaseproof (waxed) paper.

2 In a small pan, melt the butter over a medium heat, stir in the flour and cook for 1 minute, stirring. Whisk in half the milk until smooth, then whisk in the remaining milk. Add the bay leaf and seasoning. Bring to the boil and cook, stirring constantly, for 1 minute. Remove the pan from the heat and discard the bay leaf. Beat the egg yolks, one at a time, into the hot sauce, then stir in the cheese until it is completely melted. Set aside.

3 In a large bowl, whisk the egg whites slowly until they become frothy. Add the cream of tartar, then increase the speed and whisk until they form soft peaks that just flop over at the top.

4 Whisk a spoonful of beaten egg whites into the cheese sauce to lighten it. Pour the cheese sauce over the remaining whites. Using a rubber spatula or large metal spoon, gently fold the sauce into the whites, cutting down through the centre to the bottom, then along the side of the bowl and up to the top.

5 Spoon the soufflé mixture into the ramekins, filling them about three-quarters full. Put the ramekins in a shallow ovenproof dish and pour in boiling water to come halfway up the sides of the ramekins. Bake for about 18 minutes until puffed and golden brown. Let the soufflés cool in the ramekins just long enough for them to deflate.

6 Increase the oven temperature to 220°C/425°F/Gas 7. Run a knife around the edge of the soufflés and invert on to an ovenproof dish. Remove the lining paper.Lightly season the cream and pour over the soufflés, sprinkle with almonds and bake for 10–15 minutes until well risen and golden. Serve immediately, garnished with sprigs of parsley.

pancakes, scones & waffles

ingredients

175g/6oz/1½ cups **plain**
    (all-purpose) **flour,** sifted
pinch of **salt**
15ml/1 tbsp **caster**
    (superfine) **sugar**
2 large (US extra large) **eggs**
150ml/¼ pint/⅔ cup **milk**
5ml/1 tsp **bicarbonate of soda**
    (baking soda)
10ml/2 tsp **cream of tartar**
oil, for cooking
butter and **maple syrup,**
    for drizzling
crisply grilled (broiled) **bacon,**
    to serve

cook's tip
Make a batch of bitesize pancakes
in advance and freeze for
brunch parties.

american pancakes with grilled bacon

THESE LITTLE **BUTTERY** PANCAKES WILL BE
EATEN IN SECONDS, SO MAKE **PLENTY**. THE
BATTER CAN BE MADE THE NIGHT BEFORE,
READY TO COOK FOR **BREAKFAST**.

method

MAKES ABOUT 20

1 To make the batter, mix together the flour, salt and sugar in a large
    bowl. In a separate bowl, beat the eggs and milk together, then
    gradually stir into the flour, beating to a smooth, thick consistency.
    Add the bicarbonate of soda and cream of tartar, mix well, then
    cover and chill in the refrigerator until ready to cook.

2 When you are ready to cook the pancakes, beat the batter again. Heat
    a little oil in a heavy frying pan or griddle. Drop dessertspoonfuls of
    the mixture into the pan, spaced well apart, and cook over a fairly
    high heat until bubbles appear on the surface of the pancakes and the
    undersides become golden brown.

3 Carefully turn the pancakes over with a palette knife or fish slice
    (metal spatula) and cook briefly until golden underneath, then transfer
    them to a heated serving dish. Top each pancake with a little butter
    and drizzle with maple syrup. Serve with grilled bacon.

oaty pancakes with bananas & nuts

THESE **THICK** AND DELICIOUS PANCAKES ARE TOPPED WITH A **MOUTHWATERING** MIXTURE OF **MAPLE** SYRUP FLAVOURED **CARAMEL** BANANAS AND **PECAN** NUTS.

method

SERVES 4

1 To make the pancakes, mix together the plain and wholemeal flours, oats, baking powder, salt and sugar in a bowl. Make a well in the centre of the flour mixture and add the egg, oil and a quarter of the milk. Mix well, then gradually add the rest of the milk to make a thick batter. Leave to rest for 20 minutes in the refrigerator.

2 Heat a large, heavy, lightly oiled frying pan. Using about 30ml/2 tbsp of batter for each pancake, cook two to three pancakes at a time. Cook for 3 minutes on each side or until golden. Keep warm while you cook the remaining five to six pancakes.

3 To make the caramel bananas and pecan nuts, wipe out the frying pan and add the butter. Heat gently until the butter melts, then stir in the maple syrup. Add the bananas and pecan nuts to the pan.

4 Cook for about 4 minutes, turning once, or until the bananas have just softened and the sauce has caramelized. To serve, place two pancakes on each of four warm plates and top with the caramel bananas and pecan nuts. Serve immediately.

ingredients

75g/3oz/⅔ cup **plain**
    (all-purpose) **flour**
50g/2oz/½ cup **wholemeal**
    (whole-wheat) **flour**
50g/2oz/½ cup **rolled oats**
5ml/1 tsp **baking powder**
pinch of **salt**
25g/1oz/2 tbsp **caster**
    (superfine) **sugar**
1 **egg**
15ml/1 tbsp **sunflower oil**, plus
    extra for frying
250ml/8fl oz/1 cup **semi-**
    skimmed (low-fat) **milk**

For the caramel bananas and
    pecan nuts
50g/2oz/¼ cup **butter**
15ml/1 tbsp **maple syrup**
3 **bananas**, halved and
    quartered lengthwise
25g/1oz/¼ cup **pecan nuts**

ingredients

225g/8oz floury **potatoes**, cut
   into uniform chunks
115g/4oz/1 cup **plain**
   (all-purpose) **flour**, plus extra
   for dusting
2.5ml/½ tsp **salt**
2.5ml/½ tsp **baking powder**
50g/2oz/¼ cup **butter**, diced,
   plus extra for greasing
25ml/1½ tbsp **milk**
bacon rashers (strips), to serve

irish griddle scones

THESE ARE ALSO CALLED **POTATO CAKES**
OR GRIDDLE CAKES. THEY ARE DELICIOUS
SERVED **PIPING HOT**, STRAIGHT FROM THE
GRIDDLE, WITH BUTTER AND **JAM**, OR WITH
BACON FOR A HEARTY BREAKFAST.

method   MAKES 6

1 Add the potato chunks to a large pan of boiling water and cook over
   a medium heat until tender. Drain the potatoes well and return them to
   the pan over a high heat. Using a wooden spoon, stir the potatoes for
   about 1 minute until all traces of moisture have evaporated. Remove
   the pan from the heat. Mash the potatoes thoroughly, making sure
   there are no lumps.

2 Sift together the flour, salt and baking powder into a bowl. Rub in the
   diced butter with your fingertips until the mixture has the consistency
   of fine breadcrumbs.

3 Add the mashed potatoes and mix thoroughly with a fork. Make a well
   in the centre and pour in the milk, then mix to form a smooth dough.

4 Turn out on to a lightly floured surface and knead gently for about
   5 minutes until soft and pliable. Roll out to a round 5mm/¼in thick.
   Cut in half, then cut each half into 3 wedges.

5 Before you cook the scones, fry the bacon to serve with them. Keep
   warm in a low oven until the scones are ready.

6 Grease a flat griddle or heavy frying pan with a little butter and heat
   until very hot. Add the cakes and fry for 3–4 minutes until golden
   brown on both sides turning once. Serve hot with the bacon.

cheese & potato scones

THE UNUSUAL ADDITION OF **CREAMY** MASHED POTATO GIVES THESE WHOLEMEAL SCONES A **LIGHT** MOIST **CRUMB** AND A CRISP CRUST. A SPRINKLING OF MATURE **CHEDDAR** AND **SESAME SEEDS** ADDS THE FINISHING TOUCH.

ingredients

115g/4oz/1 cup **wholemeal** (whole-wheat) **flour**, plus extra for dusting

2.5ml/½ tsp **salt**

20ml/4 tsp **baking powder**

40g/1½oz/3 tbsp **unsalted** (sweet) **butter**, plus extra for greasing

2 **eggs**, beaten

50ml/2fl oz/¼ cup **semi-skimmed** (low-fat) **milk** or **buttermilk**

115g/4oz/1½ cups cooked, **mashed potato**

45ml/3 tbsp chopped **fresh sage**

50g/2oz/½ cup grated mature (sharp) **Cheddar cheese**

sesame seeds, for sprinkling

variations

Use self-raising (self-rising) flour instead of wholemeal flour and baking powder, if you wish. Fresh rosemary, basil or thyme can be used in place of the sage.

method

MAKES 9

1 Preheat the oven to 220ºC/425ºF/Gas 7. Grease a baking sheet. Sift the flour, salt and baking powder into a bowl. Rub in the butter with your fingers until the mixture resembles breadcrumbs. Mix in half the beaten eggs and all the milk or buttermilk. Add the mashed potato, sage and half the Cheddar and mix to a soft dough with your hands.

2 Turn out the dough on to a floured surface and knead lightly until smooth. Roll out the dough to 2cm/¾in thick, then stamp out 9 scones using a 6cm/2½in fluted cutter.

3 Place the scones on the prepared baking sheet and brush the tops with the remaining beaten egg. Sprinkle the rest of the cheese and the sesame seeds on top and bake for 15 minutes until golden. Transfer to a wire rack and leave to cool.

dill & potato scones

method

POTATO SCONES FLAVOURED WITH DILL ARE QUITE **SCRUMPTIOUS** AND CAN BE SERVED WARM JUST WITH BUTTER, OR IF YOU WANT TO MAKE THEM **SUBSTANTIAL** ENOUGH FOR BRUNCH, SERVE THEM TOPPED WITH FLAKED **SALMON** OR SMOKED MACKEREL.

ingredients

oil, for greasing

225g/8oz/2 cups **self-raising** (self-rising) **flour**, plus extra for dusting

40g/1½oz/3 tbsp **butter**, softened

pinch of **salt**

15ml/1 tbsp finely chopped **fresh dill**

175g/6oz/2¼ cups cooked, **mashed potato**

30–45ml/2–3 tbsp **milk**

1   Preheat the oven to 230°C/450°F/Gas 8. Grease a baking sheet. Sift the flour into a bowl, and rub in the butter with your fingertips. Add the salt and dill and stir.

2   Add the mashed potato to the mixture and enough milk to make a soft, pliable dough.

3   Turn out the dough on to a well-floured surface and roll out until it is fairly thin. Cut into rounds using a 7.5cm/3in cutter.

4   Place the scones (biscuits) on the prepared baking sheet, leaving space between them, and bake for 20–25 minutes until risen and golden. Serve warm.

> **cook's tip**
> If you don't have any dill, you can replace it with any other herb of your choice. Try fresh parsley or basil as an alternative.

savoury potato drop scones

method

THESE LIGHT SCONES HAVE A DELICIOUS **MILD MUSTARD** AND CHEESE FLAVOUR, THEY MAKE A GREAT **BREAKFAST** DISH SERVED WITH **SCRAMBLED EGGS** AND GRILLED **TOMATOES**.

ingredients

175g/6oz **floury potatoes**, diced

115g/4oz/1 cup **self-raising** (self-rising) **flour**

5ml/1 tsp **mustard powder**

1 **egg**, beaten

25g/1oz/¼ cup grated **Cheddar cheese**

150ml/¼ pint/⅔ cup **milk**

oil, for frying and greasing

salt and **ground black pepper**

butter, to serve

1   Cook the potatoes in plenty of boiling salted water for 20 minutes or until tender. Drain the potatoes and then mash them well.

2   Spoon the mashed potato from the pan into a large mixing bowl and then add the flour, mustard powder, egg, cheese and milk.

3   Beat well until the mixture comes together. Season to taste with salt and pepper.

4   Heat a flat griddle pan or heavy frying pan and brush with oil. Drop tablespoonfuls of the mixture on to the griddle or pan and cook for 1–2 minutes until golden. Flip the scones over and cook the second side. Repeat to make 16 scones. Serve warm with butter.

> **cook's tip**
> Use other strong flavoured cheeses for a change – try grated Parmesan or Red Leicester or crumbled Stilton or Roquefort.

ingredients

450g/1lb **waxy potatoes**

1 small **onion**, grated

4 **streaky** (fatty) **bacon rashers** (slices), finely chopped

30ml/2 tbsp **self-raising** (self-rising) **flour**

2 **eggs**, beaten

vegetable oil, for deep-frying

salt and **ground black pepper**

fresh parsley, to garnish

variation

For a vegetarian alternative, omit the bacon and replace it with red (bell) pepper.

savoury potato cakes

GOLDEN AND **CRISP**, BUT SOFT WHEN YOU BITE INTO THEM, THESE POTATO CAKES ARE **WONDERFUL** FOR **BREAKFAST**, WITH OR WITHOUT ANYTHING ELSE.

method

SERVES 3–4

1 Coarsely grate the potatoes, rinse, drain and pat dry on kitchen paper, then mix with the onion, half the bacon, the flour, eggs and seasoning.

2 Heat a 1cm/½in layer of oil in a heavy frying pan until really hot, then add about 15ml/1 tbsp of the potato mixture and quickly spread out the mixture with the back of the spoon, taking care that it does not break up.

3 Add a few more spoonfuls of the mixture in the same way, leaving space between them so they do not stick together, and fry them for 4–5 minutes until golden on the undersides.

4 Turn the cakes over and fry the other side. Drain on kitchen paper. Transfer to an ovenproof dish and keep warm in a low oven while frying the rest. Fry the remaining bacon and scatter with the parsley over the hot cakes.

rum & banana waffles

THESE **SCRUMPTIOUS** WAFFLES CAN BE MADE IN ADVANCE, WRAPPED TIGHTLY, **FROZEN**, AND THEN **WARMED THROUGH** IN THE OVEN JUST BEFORE SERVING.

method

MAKES 9

1 Sift the dry ingredients into a large mixing bowl. Make a well in the centre. Add the eggs, melted butter and milk. Whisk together, gradually incorporating the flour mixture, until smooth.

2 Whisk in the buttermilk and vanilla. Cover and leave to stand for 30 minutes. Preheat the oven to 150°C/300°F/Gas 2.

3 Heat a hand-held waffle iron over the heat. Stir the batter and add more milk if required (the consistency should be quite thick). Open the waffle iron and pour some batter over two-thirds of the surface. Close it and wipe off any excess batter.

4 Cook for 3–4 minutes, carefully turning the waffle iron over once during cooking. If using an electric waffle maker, follow the manufacturer's instructions for cooking.

5 When the batter stops steaming, open the iron and lift out the waffle with a fork. Put it on a heatproof plate and keep it hot in the oven. Repeat with the remaining batter to make nine waffles in all. Preheat the grill (broiler).

6 To cook the bananas, spread them out on a large shallow baking tin (pan) and top with the nuts. Sprinkle over the demerara sugar. Mix the maple syrup and rum together and spoon over. Grill (broil) for 3–4 minutes or until the sugar begins to bubble. Serve on top of the waffles with single cream.

ingredients

225g/8oz/2 cups **plain**
   (all-purpose) **flour**
10ml/2 tsp **baking powder**
5ml/1 tsp **bicarbonate of soda**
   (baking soda)
15ml/1 tbsp **caster**
   (superfine) **sugar**
2 **eggs**
50g/2oz/¼ cup **butter**, melted
175ml/6fl oz/¾ cup **milk**, plus
   extra if needed
300ml/½ pint/1¼ cups
   buttermilk
5ml/1 tsp **vanilla**
   essence (extract)
single (light) **cream**, to serve

For the bananas
6 **bananas**, thickly sliced
115g/4oz/1 cup **pecan nuts**,
   broken into pieces
50g/2oz/⅓ cup **demerara**
   (raw) **sugar**
75ml/5 tbsp **maple syrup**
45ml/3 tbsp **dark rum**

the vegetarian brunch

lentil kedgeree

THIS **SPICY** LENTIL AND RICE DISH IS A DELICIOUS **VARIATION** OF THE ORIGINAL **INDIAN** KEDGEREE, KITCHIRI. YOU CAN **SERVE** IT **AS IT IS**, OR TOPPED WITH QUARTERED HARD-BOILED **EGGS** IF YOU'D LIKE TO ADD MORE **PROTEIN**. IT IS ALSO GREAT SERVED ON LARGE GRILLED FIELD **MUSHROOM** CAPS.

ingredients

50g/2oz/¼ cup **dried red lentils**, rinsed
1 **bay leaf**
225g/8oz/1 cup **basmati rice**, rinsed
4 **cloves**
50g/2oz/¼ cup **butter**
5ml/1 tsp **curry powder**
2.5ml/½ tsp **mild chilli powder**
30ml/2 tbsp chopped fresh **flat leaf parsley**
salt and **ground black pepper**
4 **hard-boiled** (hard-cooked) **eggs**, quartered, to serve (optional)

method
SERVES 4

1 Put the lentils in a pan, add the bay leaf and cover with cold water. Bring to the boil, skim off any foam that rises to the surface, then reduce the heat. Cover and simmer for 25–30 minutes, until tender. Drain, then discard the bay leaf.

2 Meanwhile, place the rice in a pan and cover with 475ml/16fl oz/ 2 cups boiling water. Add the cloves and a generous pinch of salt. Cook, covered, for 10–15 minutes, until all the water is absorbed and the rice is tender. Discard the cloves.

3 Melt the butter over a gentle heat in a large frying pan, then add the curry and chilli powders and cook for 1 minute.

4 Stir in the lentils and rice and mix well until they are coated in the spiced butter. Season and cook for 1–2 minutes until heated through. Stir in the parsley and serve with the hard-boiled eggs, if using.

griddled tomatoes on soda bread

NOTHING COULD BE **SIMPLER** THAN THIS BREAKFAST OR BRUNCH DISH, YET A **DRIZZLE** OF OLIVE OIL AND **BALSAMIC** VINEGAR AND SHAVINGS OF **PARMESAN** CHEESE TRANSFORM IT INTO SOMETHING REALLY **SPECIAL**.

ingredients

olive oil, for brushing and drizzling
6 **tomatoes**, thickly sliced
4 thick slices **soda bread**
balsamic vinegar, for drizzling
salt and **ground black pepper**
shavings of **Parmesan cheese**, to serve

method
SERVES 4

1 Brush a griddle pan with olive oil and heat. Add the tomato slices and cook for about 4 minutes, turning once, until softened and slightly blackened. Alternatively, heat a grill (broiler) to high and line the rack with foil. Grill (broil) the tomato slices for 4–6 minutes, turning once, until softened.

2 Meanwhile, lightly toast the soda bread. Place the tomatoes on top of the toast and drizzle each portion with a little olive oil and vinegar. Season to taste with salt and pepper and serve immediately with thin shavings of Parmesan.

cook's tip
Using a griddle pan reduces the amount of oil required for cooking the tomatoes and gives them a delicious caramel flavour.

ingredients

1 medium **country-style loaf**

3 **courgettes** (zucchini),
   sliced lengthways

45ml/3 tbsp **olive oil**

250g/9oz/3⅔ cups **brown cap
   mushrooms**, thickly sliced

1 **garlic clove,** chopped

5ml/1 tsp **dried oregano**

45ml/3 tbsp **pesto**

250g/9oz **Taleggio cheese**, rind
   removed and sliced

50g/2oz/2 cups **green
   salad leaves**

courgette &
mushroom panino

THIS DELICIOUS COMBINATION OF GRILLED
COURGETTES, **GARLIC** MUSHROOMS,
TALEGGIO CHEESE AND **PESTO** PACKED
INSIDE A **CRUSTY LOAF** IS PERFECT FOR A
CROWD. IT TASTES WONDERFUL AND CAN BE
PREPARED THE DAY BEFORE – ENSURING A
RELAXED BRUNCH **PARTY**.

method   SERVES 6

1 Slice off the top third of the loaf and remove the inside of both the lid
and base, leaving a thickness of about 1cm/½in around the edge. (Use
the inside of the loaf to make breadcrumbs for another dish.)

2 Preheat the grill (broiler) to high and line the grill rack with foil. Brush
the courgettes with 15ml/1 tbsp of the olive oil, arrange on the foil-
lined rack and grill (broil) for 8–10 minutes, turning them occasionally,
until tender and browned.

3 Meanwhile, heat the remaining oil in a frying pan. Add the mushrooms,
garlic and oregano and fry for 3 minutes.

4 Arrange half the courgettes in the base of the loaf, then spread with
25ml/1½ tbsp of the pesto. Top with half the cheese and salad leaves
and all the mushroom mixture.

5 Add 1 more layer each of the remaining cheese, salad leaves and
courgettes. Spread the remaining pesto over the inside of the bread
lid and place it on top.

6 Press the lid down gently, wrap the loaf in clear film (plastic wrap) and
leave to cool. Chill in the refrigerator overnight or at least for a few
hours. Serve cut into wedges.

cannellini bean bruschetta

MORE **BRUNCH** THAN BREAKFAST, THIS DISH IS A DELICIOUS – AND **SOPHISTICATED** – VERSION OF **BEANS** ON **TOAST**.

method

SERVES 4

1 Place the beans in a large bowl and cover with water. Leave to soak overnight. Drain and rinse the beans, then place in a pan and cover with fresh water. Bring to the boil and boil rapidly for 10 minutes. Reduce the heat and simmer for 50–60 minutes or until tender.

2 While the beans are cooking, place the tomatoes in a bowl, cover with boiling water and leave for 30 seconds, then cool the tomatoes in cold water before peeling off the skins. Cut the tomatoes in half, scoop out the seeds and chop the flesh.

3 Heat the oil in a frying pan, add the fresh and sun-dried tomatoes, garlic and rosemary. Cook over a medium heat for 2 minutes until the tomatoes begin to break down and soften.

4 Drain the beans, then add the tomato mixture. Season to taste with salt and pepper and mix well.

5 Rub the cut sides of the bread slices with the garlic clove, then toast lightly. Spoon the cannellini bean mixture on top of the hot toast. Sprinkle with basil leaves, drizzle with a little extra olive oil and serve immediately.

ingredients

150g/5oz/⅔ cup **dried cannellini beans**
5 **tomatoes**
45ml/3 tbsp **olive oil**, plus extra for drizzling
2 **sun-dried tomatoes in oil**, drained and finely chopped
1 **garlic clove**, crushed
30ml/2 tbsp chopped fresh **rosemary**
salt and **ground black pepper**
a handful of fresh **basil leaves**, to garnish

To serve
12 slices Italian-style **bread**, such as **ciabatta**
1 large **garlic clove**, halved

---

cook's tip
Canned beans can be used instead of dried; use 275g/10oz/2 cups drained, canned beans and add to the tomato mixture in step 3. If the beans are canned in brine, then rinse and drain them well before use.

ingredients

60ml/4 tbsp **vegetable oil**

1 **onion**, finely chopped

450g/1lb **floury potatoes**,
    cooked and mashed

225g/8oz **cooked cabbage**
    or **Brussels sprouts**,
    finely chopped

salt and **ground black pepper**

cook's tip
If you don't have leftover cooked
cabbage or Brussels sprouts, shred
raw cabbage and cook in boiling
salted water until just tender. Drain,
then chop.

bubble & squeak

WHETHER YOU HAVE **LEFTOVERS**, OR COOK
THIS **OLD-FASHIONED** CLASSIC FROM
FRESH, BE SURE TO GIVE IT A REALLY GOOD
"**SQUEAK**" (FRY) IN THE PAN SO THE
VEGETABLES BEGIN TO **CARAMELIZE** AND
TURN A **RICH** HONEY BROWN.

method

SERVES 4

1 Heat 30ml/2 tbsp of the vegetable oil in a heavy frying pan. Add the onion and cook over a low heat, stirring frequently, until softened but not browned.

2 In a large bowl, mix together the potatoes and cooked cabbage or sprouts and season with salt and plenty of pepper to taste.

3 Add the vegetables to the pan with the cooked onions, stir well, then press the vegetable mixture into a large, even cake.

4 Cook over a medium heat for about 15 minutes until the cake is browned underneath.

5 Invert a large plate over the pan, and, holding it tightly against the pan, turn them both over together. Lift off the frying pan, return it to the heat and add the remaining vegetable oil. When hot, slide the cake back into the pan, browned side uppermost. Cook over a medium heat for 10 minutes or until the underside is golden brown. Serve hot, in wedges.

baked peppers with egg & lentils

THESE **SWEET** AND **JUICY** PEPPERS MAKE A TASTY BRUNCH DISH FOR VEGETARIANS. FOR A REALLY **HASSLE-FREE** MORNING, COOK THE LENTILS THE DAY BEFORE, THEN **SIMPLY FILL** THE PEPPERS AND TOP WITH EGG JUST BEFORE YOU COOK THEM.

method

SERVES 4

1 Put the lentils in a large pan with the turmeric, coriander, paprika and vegetable stock. Bring to the boil, stirring occasionally, and simmer for 30–40 minutes until just soft. If necessary, add a little more water during cooking.

2 Brush the outsides of the halved peppers lightly with oil and place close together on a baking sheet. Stir the chopped mint into the lentils, then fill the peppers with the mixture. Preheat the oven to 190°C/375°F/Gas 5.

3 Crack the eggs, 1 at a time, into a small jug (pitcher) and carefully pour into the middle of each pepper. Stir the egg into the lentils and sprinkle with plenty of salt and freshly ground black pepper. Bake for 10 minutes until the egg white is just set. Garnish with coriander sprigs and serve immediately.

ingredients

75g/3oz/½ cup **Puy lentils**
2.5ml/½ tsp **ground turmeric**
2.5ml/½ tsp **ground coriander**
2.5ml/½ tsp **paprika**
450ml/¾ pint/scant 2 cups
　　vegetable stock
2 large (bell) **peppers,** halved
　　lengthways and seeded
a little **oil**
15ml/1 tbsp chopped fresh **mint**
4 **eggs**
salt and **ground black pepper**
sprigs of **coriander** (cilantro),
　　to garnish

variation
Use beefsteak tomatoes instead of peppers. Cut a lid off the tomatoes and scoop out their middles using a spoon. Fill with the lentils and eggs and bake as above.

ingredients

250g/9oz/1½ cups
   bulgur wheat
4 small (US medium) **eggs**
1 **fennel bulb**
1 bunch of **spring onions**
   (scallions), chopped
25g/1oz/½ cup **drained sun-**
   dried tomatoes in oil, sliced
45ml/3 tbsp chopped
   fresh **parsley**
30ml/2 tbsp chopped **fresh mint**
75g/3oz/¾ cup **black olives**
60ml/4 tbsp **olive oil**, preferably
   Greek or Spanish
30ml/2 tbsp **garlic oil**
30ml/2 tbsp **lemon juice**
50g/2oz/½ cup chopped
   hazelnuts, toasted
1 **open-textured loaf** or
   4 pitta breads, warmed
salt and **ground black pepper**

cook's tip
If you are in a hurry, soak the bulgur
wheat in boiling water for about
20 minutes. Drain and rinse under
cold water to cool, then drain well.

egg & fennel tabbouleh with nuts

TABBOULEH IS A **MIDDLE EASTERN** SALAD
OF STEAMED **BULGUR** WHEAT, FLAVOURED
WITH PLENTY OF FRESH PARSLEY, **MINT**,
LEMON JUICE AND **GARLIC**. IT HAS A
WONDERFULLY REFRESHING, NUTTY FLAVOUR
AND IS PERFECT AT A SUMMER **BARBECUE**
BRUNCH SERVED WITH GRILLED MEATS.

method
SERVES 4

1 In a bowl, pour boiling water over the bulgur wheat and leave to soak
for about 15 minutes.

2 Drain the bulgur wheat in a metal sieve, and place the sieve over a
pan of boiling water. Cover the pan and sieve with a lid and steam for
about 10 minutes. Fluff up the grains with a fork and spread out on a
metal tray. Set aside to cool.

3 Hard-boil (hard-cook) the eggs for 8 minutes. Cool under running
water, then peel and quarter.

4 Halve and finely slice the fennel. Cook in boiling salted water for
6 minutes, drain and cool under running water.

5 Place the bulgur wheat in a large bowl and stir in the eggs, fennel,
spring onions, sun-dried tomatoes, parsley, mint and olives. Dress
with olive oil, garlic oil and lemon juice and season well. Sprinkle with
toasted hazelnuts and serve with the bread.

spinach & goat's cheese roulade

THIS **TWICE-BAKED** ROULADE IS REALLY A FLAT, ROLLED **SOUFFLÉ**. BECAUSE IT HAS AIR TRAPPED INSIDE, IT RISES AGAIN ON REHEATING AND BECOMES QUITE **CRISP** AND **GOLDEN** ON THE OUTSIDE.

method

SERVES 4

1 Preheat the oven to 190°C/375°F/Gas 5. Line a 30 × 20cm/ 12 × 8in Swiss-roll tin (jelly-roll pan) with greaseproof (waxed) paper, making sure that the edge of the paper rises well above the sides of the tin. Grease lightly.

2 Mix together the milk, flour and 50g/2oz/¼ cup of the butter in a large pan. Bring to the boil over a low heat, whisking constantly until thick and creamy. Lower the heat and simmer for about 2 minutes, then mix in the goat's cheese and half the grated Parmesan.

3 Remove the pan from the heat and leave to cool for 5 minutes, then beat in the egg yolks. Season to taste with salt and pepper.

4 Whisk the egg whites in a large bowl until soft peaks form. Carefully fold the whites into the cheese mixture, using a large metal spoon. Spoon the mixture into the prepared tin, spread gently to level, then bake for about 15 minutes until the top feels just firm.

5 Let the roulade cool for a short time. Meanwhile, sprinkle a sheet of greaseproof paper with a little Parmesan cheese and carefully invert the roulade on to the paper. Tear the lining paper away from the base of the roulade, in strips. Roll up in the greaseproof paper and set the roulade aside to cool completely.

6 To make the filling, melt the remaining butter in a pan. Remove and reserve 30ml/2 tbsp. Add the mushrooms to the pan and stir-fry for 3 minutes. In a separate pan, cook the spinach until it wilts. Drain well, add to the mushrooms and stir in the crème fraîche. Season, then cool. Preheat the oven to 190°C/375°F/Gas 5.

7 Unroll the roulade and spread over the filling. Roll it up again and place on a baking sheet. Brush with the reserved butter and sprinkle with the remaining Parmesan. Bake for 15 minutes until risen and golden. Serve immediately.

ingredients

150g/5oz/⅔ cup **butter**, plus extra for greasing

300ml/½ pint/1¼ cups **milk**

50g/2oz/½ cup **plain** (all-purpose) **flour**

100g/3¾oz **goat's cheese**, chopped

40g/1½oz/½ cup freshly grated **Parmesan cheese**, plus extra for sprinkling

4 **eggs**, separated

250g/9oz/2¼ cups fresh **shiitake mushrooms**, sliced

275g/10oz **baby spinach leaves**, washed

45ml/3 tbsp **crème fraîche**

salt and **ground black pepper**

meat & fish

ingredients

350g/12oz **unsmoked bacon**
  rashers (strips)
50g/2oz/¼ cup **unsalted**
  (sweet) **butter**, plus extra
  for spreading
115g/4oz/1½ cups **chanterelle**
  mushrooms, trimmed
  and halved
60ml/4 tbsp **sunflower oil**
4 **eggs**
4 **large baps,** split
salt and **ground black pepper**

cook's tip

Other varieties of mushroom can be
used instead of chanterelles. Try
brown cap mushrooms, chestnut
mushrooms or portabello mushrooms.

chanterelle, bacon & egg baps

THE CHANTERELLE **MUSHROOM** WITH ITS
DELICATE, SLIGHTLY FRUITY FLAVOUR AND
ALMOST MEATY **TEXTURE** COMBINES
BEAUTIFULLY WITH EGGS AND **BACON** FOR
THIS **SOPHISTICATED** BREAKFAST BAP.

method

SERVES 4

1 Place the bacon in a large non-stick frying pan and fry in its own fat
   until crisp. Transfer to a heatproof plate, cover and keep warm.

2 Melt 25g/1oz/2 tbsp of the butter in the pan, add the chanterelles
   and fry over a gentle heat until soft, without letting them colour.
   Transfer to a plate, cover and keep warm.

3 Melt the remaining butter, add the oil and heat to a moderate
   temperature. Break the eggs into the pan, two at a time, if necessary,
   and fry them, turning to cook both sides, if you like.

4 Toast the split baps, spread with butter, then top each with bacon,
   chanterelles and a fried egg. Season to taste with salt and pepper,
   add the bap lids and serve immediately.

toad-in-the-hole

THIS **WARMING** CHILDHOOD DISH HAS BECOME CLASSIC **COMFORT FOOD** AND IS **PERFECT** FOR LIFTING THE SPIRITS ON COLD DAYS. USE ONLY THE BEST **SAUSAGES** FOR THIS GROWN-UP VERSION WHICH HAS A DELICIOUS **HERBY** CHIVE **BATTER**.

method

SERVES 4

1 Preheat the oven to 220°C/425°F/Gas 7. Sift the flour into a bowl with a pinch of salt and pepper. Make a well in the centre of the flour.

2 In a bowl or jug (pitcher), whisk the eggs, with the milk and chives, if using, then pour the mixture into the well in the flour. Gradually whisk the flour into the liquid to make a smooth batter. Cover and leave to stand for at least 30 minutes.

3 Put the vegetable fat or lard into a small roasting pan and place in the oven for 3–5 minutes. Prick the sausages with a fork, then carefully add to the hot fat and cook for 15 minutes. Turn the sausages twice during cooking.

4 Pour the prepared batter over the sausages and return to the oven. Cook for about 20 minutes, or until the batter is risen and golden and the sausages are well browned. Serve immediately.

ingredients

175g/6oz/1½ cups **plain**
   (all-purpose) **flour**
2 **eggs**
300ml/½ pint/1¼ cups **milk**
30ml/2 tbsp chopped fresh
   chives (optional)
50g/2oz/¼ cup **white vegetable**
   fat or lard (shortening)
450g/1lb **Cumberland**
   sausages or **good-quality**
   pork sausages
salt and **ground black pepper**

---

cook's tip

For a young children's supper, omit the chives from the batter and cook cocktail sausages in tartlet tins (pans) until golden. Add the batter and cook for 10–15 minutes, or until puffed up and golden.

devilled kidneys
on brioche croûtes

THESE SUCCULENT **PAN-FRIED** KIDNEYS HAVE A **PEPPERY BITE**
AND A **RICH** AND CREAMY SAUCE THAT MAKES THEM THE ULTIMATE
BRUNCH TREAT. **CRISP**, SLIGHTLY **SWEET** BRIOCHE TOASTS
COMPLEMENT THEIR FLAVOUR PERFECTLY.

ingredients

8 mini **brioche slices**
25g/1oz/2 tbsp **butter**
1 **shallot**, finely chopped
2 **garlic cloves**, finely chopped
115g/4oz/1½ cups
   mushrooms, halved
1.5ml/¼ tsp **cayenne pepper**
15ml/1 tbsp **Worcestershire**
   sauce
8 **lamb's kidneys**, halved
   and trimmed
150ml/¼ pint/⅔ cup **double**
   (heavy) **cream**
30ml/2 tbsp chopped
   fresh **parsley**

method

SERVES 4

1 Preheat the grill (broiler) and toast the brioche slices until golden
   brown on both sides, and keep warm.

2 Melt the butter in the pan until it is foaming. Add the shallot, garlic
   and mushrooms, then cook for 5 minutes, or until the shallot is
   softened. Stir in the cayenne pepper and Worcestershire sauce and
   simmer for about 1 minute.

3 Add the kidneys to the pan and cook for 3–5 minutes on each side.
   Finally, stir in the cream and simmer for about 2 minutes, or until the
   sauce is heated through and slightly thickened.

4 Place the brioche croûtes on warmed serving plates and top with the
   kidneys. Sprinkle with chopped parsley and serve immediately.

---

cook's tip

If you can't find mini brioches, you can use a large brioche instead. Slice it
thickly and stamp out croûtes using a 5cm/2in round cutter. If you like, the
brioche croûtes can be fried rather than toasted. Melt 25g/1oz/2 tbsp butter in
a frying pan and fry the croûtes until crisp and golden on both sides. Remove
from the pan and drain on kitchen paper.

ingredients

115–150g/4–5oz/1–1¼ cups
medium oatmeal

10ml/2 tsp **mustard powder**

4 **herrings**, about 225g/8oz
each, cleaned, boned, heads
and tails removed

30ml/2 tbsp **sunflower oil**

8 rindless **streaky** (fatty) **bacon**
rashers (strips)

salt and **ground black pepper**

lemon wedges, to serve

---

cook's tips

Use tongs to turn the herrings so as
not to dislodge the oatmeal.
Cook the herrings two at a time, and
don't overcrowd the frying pan.

oatmeal-crusted herrings with bacon

THIS TRADITIONAL **SCOTTISH** DISH IS
HEALTHY AND NUTRITIOUS AND INCREDIBLY
TASTY. IF YOU DON'T LIKE HERRINGS, YOU
COULD USE **TROUT** OR **MACKEREL** INSTEAD.
FOR EXTRA COLOUR AND FLAVOUR, SERVE
THE FISH WITH **GRILLED TOMATOES**.

method

SERVES 4

1 In a shallow dish, mix together the oatmeal and mustard powder with
salt and pepper. Press the herrings into the mixture one at a time to
coat them thickly on both sides. Shake off the excess oatmeal mixture
and set the herrings aside.

2 Heat the oil in a large frying pan and fry the bacon until crisp. Drain
on kitchen paper and keep hot.

3 Put the herrings into the pan and fry them for 3–4 minutes on each
side, until crisp and golden brown. Serve the herrings with the streaky
bacon rashers and lemon wedges.

fried plaice with tomato sauce

THIS **SIMPLE** DISH IS ALWAYS EXTREMELY POPULAR WITH **CHILDREN** AND IS PERFECT FOR **FAMILY** BRUNCHES. IT WORKS JUST AS WELL WITH OTHER FISH SUCH AS **LEMON SOLE**, FLOUNDER OR **DABS** (THESE DO NOT NEED SKINNING), OR FILLETS OF **HADDOCK** AND **WHITING**.

method

SERVES 4

1 First make the tomato sauce. Heat the olive oil in a large pan, add the finely chopped onion and garlic and cook gently for about 5 minutes, until softened and pale golden.

2 Stir in the chopped tomatoes and tomato purée and simmer for 20–30 minutes, stirring occasionally. Season with salt and pepper and stir in the basil.

3 Spread out the flour in a shallow dish, pour the beaten eggs into another and spread out the breadcrumbs in a third. Season the fish with salt and pepper.

4 Hold a fish in your left hand and dip it first in flour, then in egg and finally in the breadcrumbs, patting the crumbs on with your right hand. (Reverse the procedure if you are left handed.)

5 Heat the butter and oil in a frying pan until foaming. Fry the fish one at a time in the hot fat for about 5 minutes on each side, until golden brown and cooked through, but still juicy in the middle.

6 Drain the fish on kitchen paper and keep hot while you fry the rest. Serve with lemon wedges and the tomato sauce, garnished with fresh basil leaves.

ingredients

25g/1oz/¼ cup **plain**
  (all-purpose) **flour**
2 **eggs**, beaten
75g/3oz/¾ cup **dried**
  breadcrumbs, preferably
  home-made
4 small **plaice**, skinned
15g/½oz/1 tbsp **butter**
15ml/1 tbsp **sunflower oil**
salt and **ground black pepper**
fresh **basil leaves**, to garnish
1 **lemon**, quartered, to serve

For the tomato sauce
30ml/2 tbsp **olive oil**
1 **red onion**, finely chopped
1 **garlic clove**, finely chopped
400g/14oz can **chopped**
  tomatoes
15ml/1 tbsp **tomato**
  purée (paste)
15ml/1 tbsp torn fresh
  basil leaves

ingredients

oil, for deep-frying

150ml/¼ pint/⅔ cup **milk**

115g/4oz/1 cup **plain**
(all-purpose) **flour**

450g/1lb **whitebait**

salt, **ground black pepper** and
cayenne pepper

cook's tip
Most whitebait are sold frozen. Thaw them before use and dry them thoroughly on kitchen paper before you add them to the milk and flour.

devilled whitebait

SERVE THESE DELICIOUSLY **CRISP** LITTLE
FISH WITH **LEMON** WEDGES AND THINLY
SLICED **BROWN BREAD** AND BUTTER.

method

SERVES 4

1 Heat the oil in a large, deep pan or deep-fryer. Pour the milk into a shallow bowl and spoon the flour into a paper bag. Season the flour with salt, ground black pepper and a little cayenne and shake to combine thoroughly.

2 Dip a handful of the whitebait into the bowl of milk, drain them well, then drop them into the paper bag. Shake the bag gently to coat the whitebait evenly in the seasoned flour. Remove the floured whitebait and set aside.

3 Repeat the dipping and shaking with the remaining fish until they have all been coated. This is the easiest method of flouring whitebait, but don't add too many at once, or they will stick together.

4 Heat the oil for deep-frying to 190°C/375°F or until a cube of stale bread, dropped into the oil, browns in 20 seconds. Add a batch of whitebait, preferably in a deep-frying basket, and fry for 2–3 minutes, until crisp and golden brown. Drain and keep hot while you fry the rest. Sprinkle with more cayenne and serve very hot.

rice cakes with smoked salmon

THESE **ELEGANT** RICE CAKES ARE MADE
USING A RISOTTO BASE. YOU COULD SKIP
THIS STAGE AND USE **LEFTOVER** SHELLFISH
OR **MUSHROOM** RISOTTO. ALTERNATIVELY,
USE LEFTOVER LONG GRAIN RICE AND ADD
EXTRA FLAVOUR WITH **SPRING ONIONS**.

method

SERVES 4

1 Heat the olive oil in a pan and fry the onion for 3–4 minutes until soft.
Add the rice and cook, stirring constantly, until the grains are
thoroughly coated in oil. Pour in the wine and stock, a little at a time,
stirring constantly over a gentle heat until each quantity of liquid has
been absorbed before adding more.

2 Drain the mushrooms and chop them into small pieces. When the rice
is tender and all the liquid has been absorbed, stir in the mushrooms,
parsley, chives, dill and seasoning. Remove the pan from the heat and
set aside for a few minutes to cool.

3 Add the beaten egg, then stir in enough of the ground rice to bind the
mixture – it should be soft, but manageable.

4 Dust your hands with ground rice and shape the mixture into four
patties, each about 13cm/5in in diameter and about 2cm/¾in thick.

5 Heat the oil in a frying pan and fry the rice cakes, in batches if
necessary, for 4–5 minutes until evenly browned on both sides. Drain
on kitchen paper and cool slightly. Serve with the sour cream, smoked
salmon, salad and asparagus spears.

ingredients

30ml/2 tbsp **olive oil**
1 medium **onion**, chopped
225g/8oz/generous 1 cup
   risotto rice
about 90ml/6 tbsp **white wine**
about 750ml/1¼ pints/3 cups **fish**
   or **chicken stock**
15g/½oz/2 tbsp dried **porcini**
   mushrooms, soaked for
   10 minutes in warm water
   to cover
15ml/1 tbsp chopped
   fresh **parsley**
15ml/1 tbsp chopped fresh **chives**
5ml/1 tsp chopped fresh **dill**
1 **egg**, lightly beaten
about 45ml/3 tbsp **ground rice**,
   plus extra for dusting
oil, for frying
60ml/4 tbsp **sour cream**
175g/6oz **smoked salmon**
salt and **ground black pepper**
radicchio and **oakleaf lettuce**,
   tossed in **French dressing**,
   and steamed **asparagus**
   spears, to serve

ingredients

800g/1¾lb **skate wings**

15ml/1 tbsp **white wine vinegar**

4 **black peppercorns**

1 fresh **thyme** sprig

175g/6oz bag of **bitter salad leaves,** such as frisée, rocket (arugula), radicchio, escarole and lamb's lettuce

1 **orange**

1 **tomatoes**, peeled, seeded and diced

For the dressing

15ml/1 tbsp **white wine vinegar**

45ml/3 tbsp **olive oil**

2 **shallots**, finely chopped

salt and **ground black pepper**

cook's tip
When peeling the orange, take care not to include any of the bitter white pith.

skate with bitter salad leaves

THIS **LIGHT** AND **ZESTY** FISH SALAD IS GREAT FOR A SUMMER BRUNCH. SERVE IT **OUTSIDE** IN THE **GARDEN** WITH PLENTY OF TOASTED FRENCH BREAD AND, FOR A **SPECIAL OCCASION**, A GLASS OF CHILLED BUCK'S FIZZ.

method

SERVES 4

1 Put the skate wings into a large shallow pan, cover with cold water and add the vinegar, peppercorns and thyme. Bring to the boil, then poach the fish gently for 8–10 minutes, until the flesh comes away easily from the cartilage.

2 Meanwhile, make the dressing. Whisk the vinegar, olive oil and shallots together in a bowl and season to taste. Tip the salad leaves into a bowl, pour over the dressing and toss well.

3 Using a zester, remove the outer rind from the orange, then peel the orange, removing all the pith. Slice into thin rounds.

4 When the skate is cooked, flake the flesh and mix it into the salad. Add the orange rind shreds, the orange slices and tomatoes, toss gently and serve.

smoked mackerel pâté

THIS SMOKY FISH PÂTÉ HAS A **WONDERFUL TEXTURE** AND MAKES A GREAT BRUNCH DISH. IT IS **INCREDIBLY EASY** TO MAKE AND CAN BE PREPARED THE DAY BEFORE – ALLOWING YOU TO REALLY **RELAX** AND **ENJOY** YOUR MEAL. SERVE WITH SLICES OF WARMED **MELBA TOAST** OR GRAINY WHOLEMEAL TOAST.

ingredients

4 **smoked mackerel fillets**, skinned
225g/8oz/1 cup **cream cheese**
1–2 **garlic cloves**, finely chopped
juice of 1 **lemon**
30ml/2 tbsp chopped fresh **chervil, parsley** or **chives**
15ml/1 tbsp **Worcestershire sauce**
salt and **cayenne pepper**
fresh **chives**, to garnish
warmed **Melba toast** or **wholemeal toast**, to serve

cook's tip
Use peppered mackerel fillets for a more piquant flavour. This pâté can be made with smoked haddock or kipper (smoked herring) fillets.

method

SERVES 6

1 Break the mackerel fillets into large pieces and put them in a food processor. Add the cream cheese, chopped garlic, lemon juice and chervil, parsley or chives.

2 Process the mixture until it is fairly smooth but still has a slightly chunky texture.

3 Add Worcestershire sauce, salt and cayenne pepper to the fish mixture to taste. Process briefly to combine, then spoon the pâté into a dish, cover with clear film (plastic wrap) and chill. Garnish with chives and serve with warmed Melba toast or wholemeal toast.

index